Personal Finance

Turning Money into Wealth

FIFTH EDITION

Workbook

Arthur J. Keown

Virginia Polytechnic Institute and State University
R.B. Pamplin Professor of Finance

Prentice Hall

Boston   New York   San Francisco
Mexico City   Montreal   Toronto   London   Madrid   Munich   Paris
Hong Kong   Singapore   Tokyo   Cape Town   Syndey

PREFACE

We have divided the *Personal Finance Workbook* into three sections. The first section of this workbook contains tear-out **worksheets** to provide a step-by-step analysis of many of the personal finance decisions examined in the textbook. You can use them for homework assignments or to guide you through actual decisions. Icons in the textbook indicate content areas, cases, and problems that utilize the worksheets. You can also find every worksheet on the text's Web site:

www.pearsonhighered.com/keown

The second section contains **Your Financial Plan**, which guides you through a series of exercises that utilize the worksheets (available in the workbook and online) and electronic calculators (found on the text's Web site:

www.pearsonhighered.com/keown

The exercises in Your Financial Plan will help you generate a basic financial plan that explores where you are today, where you want to be in the future, and what you need to do to get there. You can also find all the exercises on the text's Web site:

www.pearsonhighered.com

The third section of this workbook contains step-by-step calculator keystrokes to help you calculate important personal finance formulas.

The text's Web site contains valuable online resources, including:

* Your Financial Plan exercises
* All worksheets used in the textbook and Your Financial Plan
* All interactive calculators used in the textbook and Your Financial Plan
* Interactive Study Guide
* Internet Exercises
* Case Problems

CONTENTS

© 2010 Pearson Education, Inc.

ISBN: 0-13-607035-3

Worksheets

These financial planning worksheets provide you with the opportunity to develop and implement your own financial plan. Many of them are taken directly from figures within the text; others are checklists or worksheets not provided within the text. As you experience personal and financial changes in your life, you've got to revise your financial plan. That means that you'll be reworking these worksheets many times over throughout your life. Unfortunately, many people work themselves into a financial corner that is much easier to avoid than it is to get out of. These worksheets provide some guidance so you can avoid the pitfalls.

Once you've developed a plan, keep in mind that it's even more important to implement and actually stick to that plan. That means using common sense and moderation. Remember, your financial plan is not the goal, it is the tool you use to achieve your goal. Think of your plan as a road map. Your destination may change, and you may get lost or even go down a few dead ends, but if your road map is good enough, you'll always find your way again.

WORKSHEET 1	Personal Financial Goals Worksheet
WORKSHEET 2	Financial Objectives Worksheet
WORKSHEET 3	Job Search Worksheet
WORKSHEET 4	Balance Sheet Worksheet
WORKSHEET 5	Simplified Income Statement Worksheet
WORKSHEET 6	Storing Financial Files Worksheet
WORKSHEET 7	Budget Tracker: Personal Income Statement Worksheet
WORKSHEET 8	Worksheet for Balancing Your Checking Account
WORKSHEET 9	Worksheet for Lease Versus Purchase Decision
WORKSHEET 10	Worksheet for the Rent Versus Buy Decision
WORKSHEET 11	Worksheet for Calculating the Maximum Monthly Mortgage Loan for Which You Qualify
WORKSHEET 12	Worksheet for Estimating Life Insurance Needs
WORKSHEET 13	Worksheet for Estimating How Much Disability Insurance Coverage You Need
WORKSHEET 14	Ways to Lower Your Home Insurance Costs
WORKSHEET 15	Insurance Tracker Worksheet
WORKSHEET 16	Worksheet for Funding Your Retirement Needs
WORKSHEET 17	Worksheet for Calculation of Estate Taxes for the 2009 Tax Year
WORKSHEET 18	Starting Point Questionnaire Worksheet
WORKSHEET 19	Personal Information Worksheet
WORKSHEET 20	Your Personal Financial Goals Worksheet
WORKSHEET 21	Personal Property Inventory Worksheet
WORKSHEET 22	Beneficiaries Contact Worksheet
WORKSHEET 23	Estate Planning Worksheet
WORKSHEET 24	Assisting Parties Worksheet

W 1
orksheet

Personal Financial Goals Worksheet

Make sure your goals are realistic and stated in specific, measurable terms. In addition, prioritize your goals and identify a specific time frame within which you would like to accomplish them. The listing below is not meant to be all-inclusive, but merely to provide a framework within which goals can be formalized.

Short-Term Goals (less than 1 year)

GOAL	PRIORITY LEVEL	DESIRED ACHIEVEMENT DATE	ANTICIPATED COST
Accumulate emergency funds equal to 3 months' living expenses	_____	_____	_____
Pay off outstanding bills	_____	_____	_____
Pay off outstanding credit cards	_____	_____	_____
Purchase adequate property, health, disability, and liability insurance	_____	_____	_____
Purchase a major item	_____	_____	_____
Finance a vacation or some other entertainment item	_____	_____	_____
Other short-term goals (specify)	_____	_____	_____

Intermediate-Term Goals (1 to 10 years)

Save funds for college for an older child	_____	_____	_____
Save for a major home improvement	_____	_____	_____
Save for a down payment on a house	_____	_____	_____
Pay off outstanding major debt	_____	_____	_____
Finance very large items (weddings)	_____	_____	_____
Purchase a vacation home or time-share unit	_____	_____	_____
Finance a major vacation (overseas)	_____	_____	_____
Other intermediate-term goals (specify)	_____	_____	_____

Long-Term Goals (greater than 10 years)

Save funds for college for a young child	_____	_____	_____
Purchase a second home for retirement	_____	_____	_____
Create a retirement fund large enough to supplement your pension so that you can live at your current standard	_____	_____	_____
Take care of your parents after they retire	_____	_____	_____
Start your own business	_____	_____	_____
Other long-term goals (specify)	_____	_____	_____

2 Financial Objectives Worksheet

The generic objectives provided are typical for people of all ages and are geared to assist you with your goal setting. Please rank the objectives on the following scale.

0 – Not applicable at this time   3 – Important
1 – Not important   4 – Very important
2 – Somewhat important   5 – Crucial

Financial/Personal Objectives	0	1	2	3	4	5
Becoming more financially knowledgeable						
Improving record keeping methods						
Finding a life partner						
Starting a family						
Aquiring additional home furnishings						
Reducing revolving debt						
Increasing savings						
Reducing taxes						
Paying off student loans						
Evaluating insurance needs						
Increasing insurance protection						
Advancing in current career						
Changing careers						
Increasing investment diversification						
Increasing investment return						
Starting a small business						
Planning for children's education costs						
Saving to return to college						
Purchasing a vehicle						
Saving for the down payment on a home						
Purchasing a home						
Caring for parents						
Investing an inheritance						
Saving for retirement						
Retiring early						
Traveling extensively in retirement						
Giving to charity						
Transferring estate assets						
Other:						

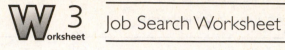

Job Search Worksheet

Notes

The Search
(Complete items 1 to 3 on this checklist before starting your job search.)

1. **Identify Occupations**
   - Make a background and experience list.
   - Review information on jobs.
   - Identify jobs that use your talents.

2. **Identify Employers**
   - Ask relatives and friends to help you look for job openings.
   - Go to your State Employment Service Office for assistance.
   - Contact employers to get company and job information.

3. **Prepare Materials**
   - Write résumés (if needed). Use job announcements to "fit" your skills with job requirements.
   - Write cover letters or letters of application.

The Daily Effort

4. **Contact Employers**
   - Call employers directly (even if they're not advertising openings). Talk to the person who would supervise you if you were hired. Make note of names.
   - Go to companies to fill out applications.
   - Contact your friends and relatives to see if they know about any openings.

The Interview
(Complete items 5 to 8 when you have interviews.)

5. **Prepare for Interviews**
   - Learn about the company you're interviewing with.
   - Review job announcements to determine how your skills will help you do the job.
   - Assemble résumés, application forms, etc. (make sure everything is neat).

6. **Go to Interviews**
   - Dress right for the interview.
   - Go alone.
   - Be neat, concise, and positive.
   - Thank the interviewer.

(continued)

Job Search Worksheet —*continued*

Notes

7. Evaluate Interviews
- Send a thank-you note to the interviewer within 24 hours of the interview.
- Think about how you could improve the interview.

8. Take Tests
- Find out about the test(s) you're taking.
- Brush up on job skills.
- Relax and be confident.

9. Accept the Job!
- Get an understanding of job duties and expectations, work hours, salary, benefits, and so on.
- Be flexible when discussing salary (but don't sell yourself short).
- *Congratulations!*

W 4 Balance Sheet—Calculating Your Net Worth
Worksheet

Assets		Value
Cash		_____
Checking	+	_____
Savings/CDs	+	_____
Money Market Funds	+	_____
Other Monetary Assets	+	_____
A. Total Monetary Assets	A. =	_____
Mutual Funds		_____
Stocks	+	_____
Bonds	+	_____
Life Insurance (cash-value)	+	_____
Cash Value of Annuities	+	_____
Investment Real Estate (REITs, partnerships)	+	_____
Other Investments	+	_____
B. Total Investments	B. =	_____
401(k) and 403(b)		_____
Company Pension	+	_____
Keogh	+	_____
IRA	+	_____
Other Retirement Plans	+	_____
C. Total Retirement Plans	C. =	_____
Primary Residence		_____
2nd Home	+	_____
Time-Shares/Condominiums	+	_____
Other Housing	+	_____
D. Total Housing (market value)	D. =	_____
Automobile 1		_____
Automobile 2	+	_____
Other Automobiles	+	_____
E. Total Automobiles	E. =	_____
Collectibles		_____
Boats	+	_____
Furniture	+	_____
Other Personal Property	+	_____
F. Total Personal Property	F. =	_____
Money Owed You		_____
Market Value of Your Business	+	_____
Other	+	_____
G. Total Other Assets	G. =	_____
H. Total Assets (add lines A through G)	H. =	_____

(continued)

4   Balance Sheet—Calculating Your Net Worth—*continued*

Liabilities or Debts	Value	
I. Current Bills (unpaid balance)	I. =	_____
Visa		_____
MasterCard	+	_____
Other Credit Cards	+	_____
J. Total Credit Card Debt	J. =	_____
First Mortgage		_____
2nd Home Mortgage	+	_____
Home Equity Loan	+	_____
Other Housing Debt	+	_____
K. Total Housing	K. =	_____
Automobile 1		_____
Automobile 2	+	_____
Other Automobile Loans	+	_____
L. Total Automobile Loans	L. =	_____
College Loans		_____
Loans on Life Insurance Policies	+	_____
Bank Loans	+	_____
Installment Loans	+	_____
Other	+	_____
M. Total Other Debts	M. =	_____
N. Total Debt (add lines I through M)	N. =	_____

Net Worth

H. Total Assets	H. +	_____
N. Less: Total Debt	N. −	_____
O. Equals: Net Worth	O. =	_____

5   Simplified Income Statement Worksheet

Your Take-Home Pay

A.	Total Income	A.	_____
B.	Total Income Taxes	− B.	_____
C.	After-Tax Income Available for Living Expenditures or Take-Home Pay (line A minus line B)	= C.	_____

Your Living Expenses

D.	Total Housing Expenditures	D.	_____
E.	Total Food Expenditures	+ E.	_____
F.	Total Clothing and Personal Care Expenditures	+ F.	_____
G.	Total Transportation Expenditures	+ G.	_____
H.	Total Recreation Expenditures	+ H.	_____
I.	Total Medical Expenditures	+ I.	_____
J.	Total Insurance Expenditures	+ J.	_____
K.	Total Other Expenditures	+ K.	_____
L.	Total Living Expenditures (add lines D through K)	= L.	_____
M.	Income Available for Savings and Investment (line C minus line L)	= M.	_____

6 Storing Financial Files Worksheet

Long-Term or Permanent Storage
(keep at home in a file cabinet or safe spot)

Tax Records (may be discarded after 6 years)   **Location**

☐ Tax returns   _____

☐ Paychecks   _____

☐ W-2 forms   _____

☐ 1099 forms   _____

☐ Charitable contributions   _____

☐ Alimony payments   _____

☐ Medical bills   _____

☐ Property taxes   _____

☐ Any other documentation   _____

Investment Records

☐ Bank records and nontax-related
    checks less than a year old   _____

☐ Safety deposit box information   _____

☐ Stock, bond, and mutual fund transactions   _____

☐ Brokerage statements   _____

☐ Dividend records   _____

☐ Any additional investment documentation   _____

Retirement and Estate Planning

☐ Copy of will   _____

☐ Pension plan documentation   _____

☐ IRA documentation   _____

☐ Keogh plan transactions   _____

☐ Social Security information   _____

☐ Any additional retirement documentation   _____

Personal Planning

☐ Personal balance sheet   _____

☐ Personal income statement   _____

☐ Personal budget   _____

☐ Insurance policies and documentation   _____

☐ Warranties   _____

☐ Receipts for major purchases   _____

☐ Credit card information
    (account numbers and telephone numbers)   _____

☐ Birth certificates   _____

(continued)

6   Storing Financial Files Worksheet —*continued*

- ❑ Rental agreement, if renting a dwelling _____
- ❑ Automobile registration _____
- ❑ Powers of attorney _____
- ❑ Any additional personal planning documentation _____

Safety Deposit Box Storage

Investment Records

- ❑ Certificates of deposit _____
- ❑ Listing of bank accounts _____
- ❑ Stock and bond certificates _____
- ❑ Collectibles _____

Retirement and Estate Planning

- ❑ Copy of will _____
- ❑ Nondeductible IRA records _____

Personal Planning

- ❑ Copy of will _____
- ❑ Deed for home _____
- ❑ Mortgage _____
- ❑ Title insurance policy _____
- ❑ Personal papers (birth and death certificates, alimony, adoption/custody, divorce, military, immigration, etc.) _____
- ❑ Documentation of valuables (videotape or photos) _____
- ❑ Home repair/improvement receipts _____
- ❑ Auto title _____
- ❑ Listing of insurance policies _____
- ❑ Credit card information (account numbers and telephone numbers) _____

Throw Out

- ❑ Nontax-related checks over a year old
- ❑ Records from cars and boats you no longer own
- ❑ Expired insurance policies on which there will be no future claims
- ❑ Expired warranties
- ❑ Nontax-related credit card slips over a year old

7 Budget Tracker: Personal Income Statement Worksheet

| | Month ——————— | | | Month ——————— | | | |
	Budget Income	Actual Income	Difference	Budget Income	Actual Income	Difference	Total Difference
INCOME							
Wages and Salaries							
Wage earner 1	___	___	___	___	___	___	___
+ Wage earner 2	___	___	___	___	___	___	___
= Total Wages and Salaries	___	___	___	___	___	___	___
+ Interest and Dividends	___	___	___	___	___	___	___
+ Royalties, Commissions, and Rents	___	___	___	___	___	___	___
+ Other Income	___	___	___	___	___	___	___
= **A. TOTAL INCOME**	___	___	___	___	___	___	___
TAXES							
Federal Income and Social Security	___	___	___	___	___	___	___
+ State Income	___	___	___	___	___	___	___
= **B. TOTAL INCOME TAXES**	___	___	___	___	___	___	___
C. AFTER-TAX INCOME AVAILABLE FOR LIVING EXPENDITURES OR TAKE-HOME PAY (LINE A MINUS LINE B)	___	___	___	___	___	___	___

	Budget Income	Actual Spending	Difference	Budget Income	Actual Spending	Difference	Total Difference
LIVING EXPENSES							
HOUSING							
Rent	___	___	___	___	___	___	___
+ Mortgage Payments	___	___	___	___	___	___	___
+ Utilities	___	___	___	___	___	___	___
+ Maintenance	___	___	___	___	___	___	___
+ Real Estate and Property Taxes	___	___	___	___	___	___	___
+ Fixed Assets—Furniture, Appliances, TV, etc.	___	___	___	___	___	___	___
+ Other Living Expenses	___	___	___	___	___	___	___
= **D. TOTAL HOUSING EXPENDITURES**	___	___	___	___	___	___	___
FOOD							
Food and Supplies	___	___	___	___	___	___	___
+ Restaurant Expenses	___	___	___	___	___	___	___
= **E. TOTAL FOOD EXPENDITURES**	___	___	___	___	___	___	___
CLOTHING AND PERSONAL CARE							
New Clothes	___	___	___	___	___	___	___
+ Cleaning	___	___	___	___	___	___	___
+ Tailoring	___	___	___	___	___	___	___
+ Personal Care—hair care	___	___	___	___	___	___	___
+ Other Clothing and Personal Care Expenses	___	___	___	___	___	___	___
= **F. TOTAL CLOTHING AND PERSONAL CARE EXPENDITURES**	___	___	___	___	___	___	___

(continued)

7

Budget Tracker: Personal Income Statement Worksheet —*continued*

	Month			Month			
	Budget Income	Actual Spending	Difference	Budget Income	Actual Spending	Difference	Total Difference
TRANSPORTATION							
Automobile Purchase	___	___	___	___	___	___	
+ Payments	___	___	___	___	___	___	
+ Gas, Tolls, Parking	___	___	___	___	___	___	
+ Automobile Registration/Tags/Stickers	___	___	___	___	___	___	
+ Repairs	___	___	___	___	___	___	
+ Other Transportation Expenses	___	___	___	___	___	___	
= G. TOTAL TRANSPORTATION EXPENDITURES	___	___	___	___	___	___	
RECREATION							
Movies, Theater, Sporting Events	___	___	___	___	___	___	
+ Club Memberships	___	___	___	___	___	___	
+ Vacations	___	___	___	___	___	___	
+ Hobbies	___	___	___	___	___	___	
+ Sporting Goods	___	___	___	___	___	___	
+ Gifts	___	___	___	___	___	___	
+ Reading Materials (books, newspapers, magazines)	___	___	___	___	___	___	
+ Other Recreation Expenses	___	___	___	___	___	___	
= H. TOTAL RECREATION EXPENDITURES	___	___	___	___	___	___	
MEDICAL EXPENDITURES							
Doctor	___	___	___	___	___	___	
+ Dental	___	___	___	___	___	___	
+ Prescription Drugs and Medicines	___	___	___	___	___	___	
= I. TOTAL MEDICAL EXPENDITURES	___	___	___	___	___	___	
INSURANCE EXPENDITURES							
Health	___	___	___	___	___	___	
+ Life	___	___	___	___	___	___	
+ Automobile	___	___	___	___	___	___	
+ Disability	___	___	___	___	___	___	
+ Liability	___	___	___	___	___	___	
+ Other Insurance Expenses	___	___	___	___	___	___	
= J. TOTAL INSURANCE EXPENDITURES	___	___	___	___	___	___	
OTHER EXPENDITURES							
Educational Expenditures	___	___	___	___	___	___	
+ Child care	___	___	___	___	___	___	
+ Other	___	___	___	___	___	___	
= K. TOTAL OTHER EXPENDITURES	___	___	___	___	___	___	
L. TOTAL LIVING EXPENDITURES (ADD LINES D THROUGH K)	___	___	___	___	___	___	___
M. INCOME AVAILABLE FOR SAVINGS AND INVESTMENT (LINE C MINUS LINE L)	___	___	___	___	___	___	___

8   Worksheet for Balancing Your Checking Account

1. Record in your check register all items that appear on the monthly statement received from the bank that have not previously been entered, for example, cash withdrawals from an ATM, automatic transfers, service charges, and any other transactions.

2. In your checking-account register, check off any deposits or credits and checks or debits shown on the monthly statement.

3. In the Deposits and Credits section below (section A), list any deposits that have been made since the date of the statement.

SECTION A: DEPOSITS AND CREDITS

DATE   AMOUNT

1.

2.

3.

4.

5.

6.   _____

Total Amount:

4. In the Outstanding Checks and Debits section below (section B), list any checks and debits issued by you that have not yet been reported on your account statement.

SECTION B: OUTSTANDING CHECKS AND DEBITS

CHECK NUMBER   AMOUNT

1.

2.

3.

4.

5.

6.

7.

Total Amount: _____

5. Write in the Ending Statement Balance provided in the monthly statement that you received from your bank. ....   _____

6. Write in the total amount of the Deposits and Credits you have made since the statement date (total of section A above). ....   + _____

7. Total the amounts in lines 5 and 6. ....   = _____

8. Write in the total amounts of outstanding Checks and Debits (total of section B above). ....   − _____

9. Subtract the amount in line 8 from the amount in line 7. This is your **Adjusted Statement Balance**. ....   = _____

If your Adjusted Statement Balance as calculated above does not agree with your Account Register Balance:

A. Review last month's statement to reconcilement to make sure any differences were corrected.

B. Check to make sure that all deposits, interest earned, and service charges shown on the monthly statement from your bank are included in your account register.

C. Check your addition and subtraction in both your account register and in this month's checking-account balance reconcilement above.

9 Worksheet for the Lease Versus Purchase Decision

Cost of Purchasing

	Your Numbers

a. Agreed-upon purchase price
b. Down payment
c. Total loan payments (monthly loan payment of _____ × __ months)
d. Opportunity cost on down payment (___% opportunity cost × ___ years × line b)
e. Less: Expected market value of the car at the end of the loan
f. **Total cost of purchasing (lines b + c + d − e)**

Cost of Leasing

g. Down payment (capitalized cost reduction) of _____ plus security deposit of ____
h. Total lease payments (monthly lease payments of _____ × __ months)
i. Opportunity cost of total initial payment (___% opportunity cost × ___ years × line g)
j. Any end-of-lease charges (perhaps for excess miles), if applicable
k. Less: Refund of security deposit
l. **Total cost of leasing (lines g + h + i + j − k)**

W10 Worksheet
Worksheet for the Rent Versus Buy Decision

The Cost of Renting

	1 year	7 years
a. Total monthly rent costs (monthly rent $____ × 12 months × no. years)	a. _____	a. _____
b. Total renter's insurance (annual renter's insurance $____ × no. years)	+ b. _____	+ b. _____
c. After-tax opportunity cost of interest lost because of having to make a security deposit (security deposit of $____ × after-tax rate of return of ____% × no. years)	+ c. _____	+ c. _____
d. **Total cost of renting (lines a + b + c)**	= d. _____	= d. _____

The Cost of Buying

	1 year	7 years
e. Total mortgage payments (monthly payments $____ × 12 months × no. years)	e. _____	e. _____
f. Property taxes on the new house (property taxes of $____ × no. years)	+ f. _____	+ f. _____
g. Homeowner's insurance (annual homeowner's insurance $____ × no. years)	+ g. _____	+ g. _____
h. Additional operating costs beyond those of renting: Maintenance, repairs, and any additional utilities and heating costs (additional annual operating costs $____ × no. years)	+ h. _____	+ h. _____
i. After-tax opportunity cost of interest lost because of having to make a down payment (down payment of $____ × after-tax rate of return of %____ × no. years)	+ i. _____	+ i. _____
j. Closing costs, including points (closing costs of $____)	+ j. _____	+ j. _____
k. Less savings: Total mortgage payments going toward the loan principal*	− k. _____	− k. _____
l. Less savings: Estimated appreciation in the value of the home *less* sales commission at the end of the period (current market value of house $____ × annual growth in house value of ____% × no. years − sales commission at end of the period of ____% × future value of house)	− l. _____†	− l. _____
m. **Equals: Total cost of buying a home for those who do not itemize (lines e + f + g + h + i + j − k − l)**	= m. _____	= m. _____

Additional *savings* to homebuyers who itemize

	1 year	7 years
n. Less savings: Tax savings from the tax-deductibility of the interest portion of the mortgage payments (total amount of interest payments made × marginal tax rate ____%)	− n. _____	− n. _____
o. Less savings: Tax savings from the tax-deductibility of the property taxes on the new house [(property taxes of $____ × marginal tax rate of ____%) × no. years]	− o. _____	− o. _____
p. Less savings: Tax savings from the tax-deductibility of the points portion of the closing costs (total points paid of $____ × marginal tax rate of ____%)	− p. _____	− p. _____
q. **Total cost of buying a home to homebuyers who itemize (line m minus lines n through p)**	= q. _____	= q. _____

Advantage of buying to those who *do not itemize* = Total cost of renting − Total cost of buying for those who *do not itemize*: if negative, rent; if positive, buy (line d − line m) .... ════ ════

Advantage of buying to those who *itemize* = Total cost of renting − Total cost of buying for those who *itemize*: if negative, rent; if positive, buy (line d − line q) .... ════ ════

*The total interest and principal payments can be calculated directly or approximated. To approximate the total annual interest payments, multiply the outstanding size of the loan by the interest rate, then multiply this by the number of years. While the approximation method works well for short time horizons, it is less accurate for longer time horizons.

†*Note:* If you only own the home for 1 year, the value here may be negative, meaning the sales commission is greater than the appreciation in home value. If this is the case, this is an additional cost, not a savings, and we are subtracting a negative—in effect, adding in the cost of buying the house.

W 11
Worksheet

Worksheet for Calculating the Maximum Monthly Mortgage Loan for Which You Qualify

---

METHOD 1 Determine your maximum monthly mortgage payment using the ability to pay, PITI ratio.

a. Monthly income (annual income divided by 12)   _____

b. Times 0.28: Percentage of PITI (principal, interest, taxes, and insurance) to your monthly gross income that lenders will lend in the form of a mortgage loan (multiply line a by 0.28)   × 0.28 = _____

c. Less: Estimated monthly real estate tax and insurance payments   − _____

d. Equals: Your maximum monthly mortgage payment using the 28% of PITI ratio   = _____

   To Determine the Maximum Mortgage Loan Level Using the Maximum Monthly Mortgage Payments as Determined Using the PITI Ratio (line d):

   Step 1: Monthly mortgage payment for a $10,000 mortgage with a ____ year maturity and a ____ % interest rate (using Table 8.1)   = _____

   Step 2: Maximum mortgage level = maximum monthly mortgage payment (line d) divided by the monthly mortgage payment on a $10,000, ____ %, ____ year mortgage (step 1 above) times $10,000 = (line d/step 1) × $10,000   = _____

METHOD 2 Determine your maximum monthly mortgage payment using the ability to pay, PITI plus other fixed monthly payments, ratio.

e. Monthly income (annual income divided by 12)   _____

f. Times 0.36: Percentage of PITI + current monthly fixed payments to your monthly gross income that lenders will lend in the form of a mortgage loan (multiply line e by 0.36)   × 0.36 = _____

g. Less: Current nonmortgage debt payments on debt that will take over 10 months to pay off and other monthly legal obligations such as child support and alimony payments   − _____

h. Less: Estimated monthly real estate tax and insurance payments   − _____

i. Equals: Your maximum monthly mortgage payment using the 36% of PITI + other fixed monthly payments ratio (line f - g- h)   = _____

   To Determine the Maximum Mortgage Loan Using the PITI Plus Other Fixed Monthly Payments Ratio (line i):

   Step 1: Monthly mortgage payment for a $10,000 mortgage with a ____ year maturity and a ____ % interest rate (using Table 8.1)   = _____

   Step 2: Maximum mortgage level = maximum monthly mortgage payment (line i) divided by the monthly mortgage payment on a $10,000, ____ %, ____ year mortgage (step 1 above) times $10,000 = (line i/step 1) × $10,000   = _____

METHOD 3 Determine your maximum mortgage level using the "80% of the Appraised Value of the House" rule.

j. Funds available for down payment and closing costs   _____

k. Less: Closing costs   − _____

l. Equals: Funds available for the down payment   = _____

m. Times 4: Maximum mortgage level using the "80% of the appraised value of the house" rule (the 20% down, line l, times 4 equals the 80% you can borrow)   × 4 = _____

Conclusion: **Maximum Mortgage Level for Which You Will Qualify (the lower of the amounts using method 1, method 2, or method 3)**   = _____

12 Worksheet for Estimating Life Insurance Needs

                                                                Total Needs

Step 1: Immediate Needs—Cleanup Funds

Final Illness Costs (assumed equal to your health insurance deductible)	a. _____
Estate Administration Costs (assumed equal to 4% of your assets)	+ b. _____
Burial Costs	+ c. _____
Federal Estate Taxes (if any due)	+ d. _____
State Estate Taxes	+ e. _____
Additional Legal Fees	+ f. _____
Other Immediate Needs	+ g. _____
Total Immediate Needs (add lines a through g)	= h. _____

Step 2: Debt Elimination Funds

Credit Card and Consumer/Installment Debt	i. _____
Auto Debt Outstanding	+ j. _____
Desired Mortgage Reduction	+ k. _____
Other Debt to Be Paid Off at Your Death	+ l. _____
Total Debt Elimination Funds (add lines i through l)	= m. _____

Step 3: Immediate Transitional Funds

Schooling Expenses for Surviving Spouse	n. _____
Child Care and Housekeeping Expenses	+ o. _____
Other Transitional Needs	+ p. _____
Total Immediate Transitional Funds (add lines n through p)	= q. _____

Step 4: Dependency Expenses (family needs while children are in school and dependent on family support)

Current Household Expenses (estimated as income less savings)	r. _____
Less: Deceased's Expenses (estimated as 30% of line r if surviving family includes only one member, 26% for a surviving family of two, 22% for a surviving family of three, and dropping 2% more for each additional family member)	− s. _____
Less: Spousal Income	− t. _____
Less: Social Security Survivors' Benefits	− u. _____
Less: Pension Benefits and Income	− v. _____
Equals: Income to Be Replaced Until Children Are Self-Supporting (line r − lines s through v)	= w. _____

(continued)

Worksheet for Estimating Life Insurance Needs— *continued*

Total Dependency Expenses or Money in Today's Dollars Needed for Dependency Expenses (assuming the children have *n* years until they become self-supporting and you can earn an *i*% after-tax and after-inflation return on your investments) (line w $\times$ PVIFAi$_{\%, n\ yr}$) = (____ $\times$ PVIFA$_{\_\_\%, \_\_yr}$) = (____ $\times$ ____) = x. _____

Step 5: Spousal Life Income (spousal needs after children are self-supporting)

Desired Spousal Income y. _____

Total Spousal Life Income or Money in Today's Dollars to Provide for Desired Spousal Income (assuming *n* years until the children become self-supporting and *m* years until the spouse qualifies for Social Security or retirement income, and assuming you can earn an *i*% after-tax and after-inflation return on your investments)
[line y $\times$ (PVIFAi$_{\%, n\ yr}$ − PVIFAi$_{\%, n\ yr}$)] =
[____ $\times$ (PVIFA$_{\_\_\%, \_\_yr}$ − PVIFA$_{\_\_\%, \_\_yr}$)] =
[____ $\times$ (____ − ____)] = z. _____

Step 6: Educational Expenses for Your Children

Total Educational Expenses (private school needs plus total college needs) aa. _____

Step 7: Retirement Income

Additional Desired Annual Income at Retirement bb. _____

Total Retirement Income or Money in Today's Dollars to Provide for Desired Retirement Income (assuming retirement in *m* years and desiring the additional income for *p* additional years, and assuming you can earn an i% after-tax and after-inflation return on your investments)
[line bb $\times$ (PVIFA$_{i\%, m+ p\ yr}$ − PVIFA$_{i\%, m\ yr}$)] =
[____ $\times$ (PVIFA$_{\_\_\%, \_\_yr}$ − PVIFA$_{\_\_\%, \_\_yr}$)] =
[____ $\times$ (____ − ____)] = cc. _____

Step 8: Total Funds Needed in Today's Dollars to Cover Needs

Total   (lines h + m + q + x + z + aa + cc) = dd. _____

Step 9: Assets and Insurance Available to Cover Needs

Cash from Current Insurance Policies ee. _____
Retirement Savings and Investments ff. _____
Other Assets gg. _____
Total Assets (add lines ee + ff + gg) = hh. _____

Step 10: Additional Insurance Needs

Additional Insurance Needs (line dd − line hh) = _____

Worksheet for Estimating How Much Disability Insurance Coverage You Need

1. Current monthly after-tax job-related income* _____
2. Existing disability coverage on an *after-tax-basis*
   - Social Security benefits† _____
   - Disability insurance from employer   + _____
   - Veterans' benefits and other federal
     and state disability insurance   + _____
   - Other disability coverage in place   + _____

   Total existing coverage   = _____

3. Added disability coverage needed to maintain
   current level of after-tax job-related income in
   the event of a disability (subtract 2 from 1) _____

Note: We haven't included workers' compensation disability benefits because they accompany only work-related injuries.

*Keep in mind that your investment income won't stop with a disability. Only your income from working will stop. Thus, only the portion of your income from working that you rely upon to maintain your current standard of living must be replaced. This may also include savings for such goals as your children's college education and other goals. However, you should keep in mind that your goals will generally change substantially if you are permanently disabled.

†To get an estimate of what these benefits might be, you can call the Social Security Administration at 800-772-1213 for a Personal Earnings and Benefits Estimate Statement.

Ways to Lower Your Home Insurance Costs

- ☐ Shop around.
- ☐ Raise your deductible.
- ☐ Buy your home and auto policies from the same insurance company.
- ☐ When you buy a home, buy a new one and choose the location wisely.
- ☐ Insure your house, not the land.
- ☐ Beef up your home security.
- ☐ Stop smoking.
- ☐ Ask about discounts for seniors.
- ☐ See if you can get group coverage.
- ☐ If you stay with the same insurance company—if you've kept your coverage with a company for several years—you may receive a discount for long-standing policyholders.

Source: U.S. Office of Consumer Affairs, *Consumers Resource Handbook,* 2000.

W15 Insurance Tracker Worksheet

Life Insurance: Policy 1

Company: _____   Policy Number: _____

Name of Contact: _____   Phone Number: _____

If employer provided, Pretax Premium: $ _____   Individual Premium: $ _____

Current Coverage: $ _____   Adequate: Yes ❑   No ❑

Proposed Coverage: $ _____   Additional Premium: $ _____

Life Insurance: Policy 2

Company: _____   Policy Number: _____

Name of Contact: _____   Phone Number: _____

If employer provided, Pretax Premium: $ _____   Individual Premium: $ _____

Current Coverage: $ _____   Adequate: Yes ❑   No ❑

Proposed Coverage: $ _____   Additional Premium: $ _____

Life Insurance: Policy 3

Company: _____   Policy Number: _____

Name of Contact: _____   Phone Number: _____

If employer provided, Pretax Premium: $ _____   Individual Premium: $ _____

Current Coverage: $ _____   Adequate: Yes ❑   No ❑

Proposed Coverage: $ _____   Additional Premium: $ _____

Health Insurance: Policy 1

Company: _____   Policy Number: _____

Name of Contact: _____   Phone Number: _____

If employer provided, Pretax Premium: $ _____   Individual Premium: $ _____

Current Coverage: $ _____   Adequate: Yes ❑   No ❑

Proposed Coverage: $ _____   Additional Premium: $ _____

Health Insurance: Policy 2

Company: _____   Policy Number: _____

Name of Contact: _____   Phone Number: _____

If employer provided, Pretax Premium: $ _____   Individual Premium: $ _____

Current Coverage: $ _____   Adequate: Yes ❑   No ❑

Proposed Coverage: $ _____   Additional Premium: $ _____

Disability Insurance: Policy 1

Company: _____   Policy Number: _____

Name of Contact: _____   Phone Number: _____

If employer provided, Pretax Premium: $ _____   Individual Premium: $ _____

Current Coverage: $ _____   Adequate: Yes ❑   No ❑

Proposed Coverage: $ _____

(continued)

Insurance Tracker Worksheet —*continued*

Disability Insurance: Policy 2

Company:	Policy Number:
Name of Contact:	Phone Number:
If employer provided, Pretax Premium: $	Individual Premium: $
Current Coverage: $	Adequate: Yes ❏ No ❏
Proposed Coverage: $	Additional Premium: $

Long-Term Care Insurance Policy:

Company:	Policy Number:
Name of Contact:	Phone Number:
If employer provided, Pretax Premium: $	Individual Premium: $
Current Coverage: $	Adequate: Yes ❏ No ❏
Proposed Coverage: $	Additional Premium: $

Homeowner's or Renter's Insurance Policy:

Company:	Policy Number:
Name of Contact:	Phone Number:
If employer provided, Pretax Premium: $	Individual Premium: $
Current Coverage: $	Adequate: Yes ❏ No ❏
Proposed Coverage: $	Additional Premium: $

Auto Insurance Policy:

Company:	Policy Number:
Name of Contact:	Phone Number:
If employer provided, Pretax Premium: $	Individual Premium: $
Current Coverage: $	Adequate: Yes ❏ No ❏
Proposed Coverage: $	Additional Premium: $

Other Insurance Policy:

Company:	Policy Number:
Name of Contact:	Phone Number:
If employer provided, Pretax Premium: $	Individual Premium: $
Current Coverage: $	Adequate: Yes ❏ No ❏
Proposed Coverage: $	Additional Premium: $

16 Worksheet for Funding Your Retirement Needs

Your Numbers

Step 1: Estimate your annual needs at retirement.

A. Present level of your living expenditures on an after-tax basis   _____

B. Times 0.80 equals: Base retirement expenditure level in today's dollars   × 0.80 = _____

C. Plus or minus: Anticipated increases or decreases in living expenditures
after retirement   + or − _____

D. Equals: Annual living expenditures at retirement in today's dollars on an
after-tax basis   = _____

E. Before-tax adjustment factor, based on an average tax rate of _____ % : (If the
average tax rate is not known, it can be estimated using Table 16.2, The Average
Tax Rate.) This is used to calculate the before-tax income necessary to cover
the annual living expenses in line D. Thus, line F, the before-tax income = line D/line E
where line E = (1 − Average Tax Rate)   = _____

F. Equals: The before-tax income necessary to cover the annual living
expenses in line D   Line D divided by Line E = _____

Step 2: Estimate your income available at retirement.

G. Income from Social Security in today's dollars   _____

H. Plus: Projected pension benefits in today's dollars   + _____

I. Plus: Other income in today's dollars   + _____

J. Equals (lines G + H + I): Anticipated retirement income, in today's dollars   = _____

Step 3: Calculate the (annual) inflation-adjusted shortfall.

K. Anticipated shortfall in today's dollars (line F minus line J)   = _____

L. Inflation adjustment factor, based on an anticipated inflation rate of _____ %
between now and retirement with _____ years to retirement
(*FVIFs* are found in Appendix A):
$FVIF_{\text{inflation rate \%, no. years to retirement}}$ × _____

M. Equals: Inflation-adjusted shortfall (line K × line L)   = _____

Step 4: Calculate the total funds needed at retirement to cover this shortfall over the number of years you expect to be retired (assuming an inflation-adjusted return of _____ % [return (_____ %) minus the inflation rate (_____%)] during your retirement period, with retirement anticipated to last for _____ years).

N. Calculate the funds needed at retirement to cover the inflation-adjusted shortfall over the
entire retirement period, assuming that these funds can be invested at _____ % and that the
inflation rate over this period is _____ %. Thus, determining the present value of a _____-year
annuity assuming a _____ % inflation-adjusted return: $PVIFA_{\text{inflation-adjusted return, no. years in retirement}}$
(*PVIFAs* are found in Appendix D).   _____

O. Equals: Funds needed at retirement to finance the shortfall
(line M × line N)   × line M = _____

Step 5: Determine how much you must save annually between now and retirement (_____ years until retirement and earning _____ %) to cover the shortfall.

P. Future value interest factor for an annuity for _____ years, given a _____ % expected
annual return: $FVIFA_{\text{expected rate of return, no. years to retirement}}$ (*FVIFAs* are found in Appendix C).   = _____

Q. Equals: *PMT*, or the amount that must be saved annually for _____ years
and invested at _____ % in order to accumulate the line O amount at the
end of _____ years   line O divided by line P = _____

W17 Worksheet Worksheet for Calculation of Estate Taxes for the 2009 Tax Year

	Amount	Total Amount
Step 1: Calculate the value of the _gross estate_.		
A. Value of gross estate		_____
Step 2: Calculate your _taxable estate_.		
Less:		
Funeral expenses	_____	
Estate administration expenses	+ _____	
Debt	+ _____	
Taxes	+ _____	
Marital deduction	+ _____	
Charitable deduction	+ _____	
Total		− _____
Equals:		
B. Taxable estate		= _____
Step 3: Calculate your _gift-adjusted taxable estate_.		
Plus:		
Cumulative taxable lifetime gifts (in excess of annual tax-free gift allowance per person)		+ _____
Less:		
Estate tax-free transfer threshold		− _____
Equals:		
C. Gift-adjusted taxable estate		= _____
Step 4: Calculate your estate taxes.		
Gift-adjusted taxable estate × 0.45		_____

Starting Point Questionnaire Worksheet

1. How would you describe your housing situation?
   (e.g., rent, own, live with parents, roommates)

   _____

   _____

2. What will be your primary mode of transportation?
   (e.g., personal auto, carpool, public transportation)

   _____

   _____

3. How would you describe your relationship, marriage, or family plans?
   (e.g., single, married, children)

   _____

   _____

4. How would you describe your career field (e.g., engineering, medical, sales)
   and anticipated job title? (e.g., clerk, manager, vice president)

   _____

   _____

5. What type of fringe benefits would you anticipate receiving?
   (e.g., retirement plans, insurance, vacation time)

   _____

   _____

6. What do you anticipate your first year income to be?

   _____

   _____

7. How much business travel do you anticipate? (none, 2 weeks per year, frequent)

   _____

   _____

8. How much personal travel do you anticipate? (none, 2 weeks per year, frequent)

   _____

   _____

9. Do you plan to continue your education?

   _____

   _____

10. In what types of recreational activities or hobbies will you participate?
    (e.g., sports, woodworking, hiking, etc.)

    _____

    _____

11. What types of household furnishings, electronics, and equipment do you antici-
    pate purchasing during the target year of your Financial Vision? (e.g., bedroom
    suite, refrigerator, television, etc.)

    _____

    _____

19 Personal Information Worksheet

Personal Information

Name: _____ Date: _____

Address: _____

_____

Telephone (home): _____ Fax: _____

Marital Status: ❏ Single   ❏ Married   ❏ Divorced   ❏ Widowed   ❏ Other

Name of Spouse: _____

   Date of Birth Self: _____ Spouse: _____

   Citizenship Self: _____ Spouse: _____

Names of Children:

1. _____ Date of Birth: _____

2. _____ Date of Birth: _____

3. _____ Date of Birth: _____

4. _____ Date of Birth: _____

Names of Other Dependents:

1. _____ Date of Birth: _____

2. _____ Date of Birth: _____

Financial Information

Occupation of Self: _____ Occupation of Spouse: _____

   Employer: _____   Employer: _____

   Duration: _____   Duration: _____

   Address: _____   Address: _____

   Phone: _____   Phone: _____

   Salary: $ _____   Salary: $ _____

Other Sources of Income:

1. _____ Amount: $ _____

2. _____ Amount: $ _____

3. _____ Amount: $ _____

W20 Worksheet   Your Personal Financial Goals Worksheet

Goals	Priority Level (0–5)	Target Date or Time Horizon	Current Total Cost	Future Anticipated Total Cost	Rate of Return*	Required Savings (Annual, if multiyear)
Short-Term Goals (less than 1 year)						
Intermediate-Term Goals (1 to 10 years)						
Long-Term Goals (more than 10 years)						

* The rate of return for a debt reduction goal would be the interest rate of the term loan or revolving credit line.

W21 Personal Property Inventory Worksheet

This worksheet is not intended to be an exhaustive list. For insurance purposes you should itemize the list more carefully. However, this document provides a starting point and should provide at least a minimum of documentation. The best method of cataloging your personal possessions is by narrated videotape or photographs.

Rooms / Inventory	Original Purchase Cost	Purchase Date (Mo./Yr.)	Replacement Cost (only if incurring a loss)
Living Room			
Furniture			
Electronics			
Accessories			
Other			
Dining Room			
Furniture			
Artwork			
Accessories			
Sterling Silver/Pewterware			
China			
Crystal			
Other			
Family Room			
Furniture			
Electronics			
Accessories			
Other			
Kitchen			
Furniture			
Electronics			
Accessories			
Appliances			
Other			
Den/Home Office			
Furniture			
Electronics			
Accessories			
Other			
Library/Bedroom 4			
Furniture			
Electronics			
Accessories			
Books			
Other			
Master Bedroom			
Furniture			
Electronics			
Clothing			
Jewelry			
Other			

(continued)

21 Personal Property Inventory Worksheet—*continued*

Rooms / Inventory	Original Purchase Cost	Purchase Date (Mo./Yr.)	Replacement Cost (only if incurring a loss)
Bedroom 2			
Furniture			
Electronics			
Accessories			
Clothing			
Other			
Bedroom 3			
Furniture			
Electronics			
Accessories			
Clothing			
Other			
Basement			
Furniture			
Electronics			
Accessories			
Appliances			
Other			
Attic			
Furniture			
Luggage			
Accessories			
Other			
Laundry/Utility Room			
Furniture			
Appliances			
Linens/Towels			
Other			
Garage			
Tools			
Machinery			
Sporting goods			
Other			
Collectibles			
Coins / Stamps			
Artwork			
Firearms			
Other			
Cash / postage stamps			
Total Value	$	$	

22 Beneficiaries Contact Worksheet

Name: _____ Relation: _____

Bequest: _____

Address: _____ Phone number: _____

Name: _____ Relation: _____

Bequest: _____

Address: _____ Phone number: _____

Name: _____ Relation: _____

Bequest: _____

Address: _____ Phone number: _____

Name: _____ Relation: _____

Bequest: _____

Address: _____ Phone number: _____

Name: _____ Relation: _____

Bequest: _____

Address: _____ Phone number: _____

Name: _____ Relation: _____

Bequest: _____

Address: _____ Phone number: _____

Name: _____ Relation: _____

Bequest: _____

Address: _____ Phone number: _____

Name: _____ Relation: _____

Bequest: _____

Address: _____ Phone number: _____

23 Estate Planning Worksheet

Do you and the members of your family know the location of . . .

❏ Your will, durable power of attorney, and living will (with the name of the attorney who drafted them)?

_____

_____

❏ The name of your attorney?

_____

_____

❏ Your letter of last instructions, including burial requests and organ donor information?

_____

_____

❏ Your Social Security number?

_____

_____

❏ Your safety deposit box and the key to it?

_____

_____

❏ A record of what is in your safety deposit box?

_____

_____

❏ Your birth certificate?

_____

_____

❏ Your marriage certificate?

_____

_____

❏ Any military discharge papers?

_____

_____

(continued)

Estate Planning Worksheet—*continued*

❏　Insurance policies (life, health, and property/liability), along with the name of your insurance agent?

_____

_____

❏　Deeds and titles to property (both real estate and real, for example, automobiles)?

_____

_____

❏　Your stocks, bonds, and other securities, and who your broker is?

_____

_____

❏　Any business agreements, including any debts owed you?

_____

_____

❏　All checking, savings, and brokerage account numbers, along with the location of those accounts?

_____

_____

❏　The name of your accountant?

_____

_____

❏　Your last year's income tax return?

_____

_____

❏　The name of past employers, along with any pension or retirement benefits information?

_____

_____

You should also
1.　Calculate the size of your estate.
2.　Estimate how much of your estate would be lost to taxes if you died.
3.　Know who the executor of your will is and who your beneficiaries are.
4.　Select a guardian for your children if they are under 18.

W24 Assisting Parties Worksheet

Executor of will:

Name: _____   Relation: _____

Address: _____   Phone number: _____

Co-executor of will:

Name: _____   Relation: _____

Address: _____   Phone number: _____

Power of attorney:

Name: _____   Relation: _____

Address: _____   Phone number: _____

Contingent or co-power of attorney:

Name: _____   Relation: _____

Address: _____   Phone number: _____

Health care proxy:

Name: _____   Relation: _____

Address: _____   Phone number: _____

Contingent or co-health care proxy:

Name: _____   Relation: _____

Address: _____   Phone number: _____

Guardian for minor children:

Name: _____   Relation: _____

Address: _____   Phone number: _____

Lawyer:

Name: _____   Relation: _____

Law Firm: _____

Address: _____   Phone number: _____

Trustee:

Type of trust: _____   Date of execution: _____

Name: _____   Relation: _____

Address: _____   Phone number: _____

Trustee:

Type of trust: _____   Date of execution: _____

Name: _____   Relation: _____

Address: _____   Phone number: _____

An Introduction to Your Financial Future

Getting Started on Your Financial Plan

The foundation of financial planning is controlled spending—spending that balances the needs and wants of today and tomorrow—combined with savings to accomplish your goals. Your Financial Plan is the first opportunity to apply what you have learned to your own situation—not a hypothetical case. Keep in mind that applying what you learn to *you* means a multitude of "what if" questions that are otherwise controlled for in a case. And only you can answer those "what if" questions!

Your Financial Plan guides you through a series of exercises that will, when you record them in the Master Plan Calculator (found on the text's Web site, **www.pearson highered.com/keown**) for your target year, generate a very basic financial plan. The plan will account for all of your income, living expenses, and to the extent possible, funding for future goals such as retirement.

Go to **www.pearsonhighered.com/keown** for tools and resources to help you develop Your Financial Plan.

Overview of Your Financial Plan

The exercises in Your Financial Plan match the five parts of the text. Each exercise is based on four of the five steps of the financial planning process outlined in Chapter 1. These steps include:

1. Evaluate Your Financial Health
2. Define Your Financial Goals
3. Develop a Plan of Action
4. Implement Your Plan
5. Review Your Progress, Reevaluate, and Revise Your Plan

In Part 1 you will project your uncommitted expenses (the annual costs of daily living), but as you add in savings for goals in Part 2, the cost of insurance premiums in Part 3, and savings for retirement in Part 5, you may find that there's simply not enough money to go around. It will be time for Step 5: Review Your Progress, Reevaluate, and Revise Your Plan by making adjustments. Because this is the step you will perform over and over throughout the remainder of your financial life, get into the habit of periodically reviewing, reevaluating, and revising as you work through the exercises. Once you have completed Your Financial Plan, you will be better prepared to balance your spending needs with the saving and investing strategies you need to make your dreams come true.

As you analyze your financial situation and develop your plan, you will be introduced to Excel™-based worksheets, online calculators, and recommended informational Internet sites. All of these tools are available on the text's Web site, **www.pearson highered.com/keown**.

Excel™-Based Worksheets and Calculators

We have developed these worksheets and calculators specifically for this program. Always input your data in the yellow highlighted cells. Some data will automatically fill in cells on adjoining pages. Many worksheets include embedded comment boxes with additional directions or feedback (in a red font) to guide you. If you are unsure of what data to enter in a particular place, first scan the worksheet for directions and then return to the text for further guidance.

The Master Plan Calculator serves as the foundation of your plan and you will access it frequently to store and summarize your information. You will use other worksheets, calculators, Internet sites, and your own personal research to find needed data. For example, how much will cable or satellite television cost during your target year, or how much will your student loan or auto payments cost? You'll need answers to all those questions, so save the Master Plan Calculator and periodically enter your information. To execute the files, you will also need Excel™ or another spreadsheet program that will translate Excel™ files.

Financial Calculators

The financial calculators include instructions and glossary terms to guide you. Remember, however, that as you use the calculators or worksheets you will have to make some assumptions about your financial situation or future economic conditions, just as a professional financial planner would do. Although none of your assumptions may become reality, these "educated" guesses are the closest things to facts you have. For help, consult your instructor.

Internet Sites

We have provided the Internet sites for external research to help you tailor the information you need to your situation. Although there are many other relevant sites available, these specific sites should provide the necessary information to complete Your Financial Plan.

We have included all worksheets in this workbook, and you can print completed calculators for future reference or for inclusion in Your Financial Plan. We recommend that you use a large folder or three-ring binder to maintain your work in an orderly fashion.

Your Target Year

Your target year is the 12-month period on which you base your financial plan. You can create Your Financial Plan using your current situation, but you could also decide that you want Your Financial Plan to reflect your first year of professional employment. In that case, you should treat all of your goals, income, and cost projections as if you were currently living in your target year. Base your income on the amount you could earn in your chosen career (or as a graduate student) and plan for expenses as if you were incurring them "today."

Some of you are "20-something" college students who have given little, if any, thought to making ends meet after graduation. Others of you may be professionally employed and are taking this course to learn more about your current finances. It will take initiative to work through the process, research the needed information, and analyze your situation. But regardless of your situation, the exercises in Your Financial Plan will help you explore where you are today, where you want to be in the future, and what you need to do to get there.

YOUR
FINANCIAL
PLAN

PART I

Financial Planning

Exercise I   Career and Financial Future Orientation

OBJECTIVES
By completing this part of Your Financial Plan, you will:
- Complete the Starting Point Questionnaire.
- Complete the Personal Information Worksheet.

Step 1:   Evaluate your financial health.

To begin documenting your financial life, review the Starting Point Questionnaire Worksheet (**WORKSHEET 18**) for your target year and begin answering any questions that you may already know.

Step 2:   Define your financial goals.

In addition to considering the Starting Point Questionnaire Worksheet (**WORKSHEET 18**) you will need to review the Personal Information Worksheet (**WORKSHEET 19**) to start narrowing down your most likely job, salary, and location. If you do not already have accurate information about your future compensation, research the salary offered in your chosen career field. Speak with someone working in the industry, talk with a recent graduate in your major, consult your career advisor, or use the Internet sites you will find at **www.pearsonhighered.com/keown** to research this information. In addition to salary information, you must also consider other sources of income such as commissions or bonus schedules and your benefit package, which we will consider in detail in later parts of Your Financial Plan.

While you are thinking about salary and location, you need to consider how your chosen job location may impact your ability to achieve other goals. For example, how will the area you live in affect your ability to buy a house?

Step 3:   Develop a plan of action.

Complete the Starting Point Questionnaire Worksheet and the Personal Information Worksheet with a realistic picture of your target year. You can probably project the city or town, your family status, and your job title, although the exact company may be unknown. Be as detailed as possible as this information will guide the rest of your plan and establish the context and background for your target year and, if applicable, for a spouse, partner, or friend with whom you are sharing resources.

Step 4:   Implement your plan.

Now that you have a starting point for the target year of Your Financial Plan, the only thing left is the journey. During the remaining parts of Your Financial Plan, you will have the opportunity to explore each area of financial planning as it pertains to you and your projected target year. The insight and knowledge you gain through these exercises will be of value long into your future.

Step 5: **Review your progress, reevaluate, and revise your plan.**

Remember your priorities!

Exercise 2 Financial Objectives and Goal Setting

OBJECTIVES
By completing this part of Your Financial Plan, you will:
- Establish and prioritize short-, intermediate-, and long-term goals.
- Complete the Financial Objectives and Personal Financial Goals worksheets.

Step 1: **Evaluate your financial health.**

With the context of your target year in mind, it's time to start thinking about personal and financial goals for your future. Begin by completing the Financial Objectives Worksheet (**WORKSHEET 2**) to broaden your thinking about your short-, intermediate-, and long-term goals as discussed in Chapter 1 of the text.

Step 2: **Define your financial goals.**

Once you have considered all of this information, categorize your goals by time horizon and priority as you complete the first and second columns of the Your Personal Financial Goals Worksheet (**WORKSHEET 20**). Refer to your Financial Objectives Worksheet, as needed, for assistance. As you continue to develop Your Financial Plan, you may need to revisit these goals and change the priority level, time horizon, or even the cost of the goal, but it is very important to initially codify your dreams.

Step 3: **Develop a plan of action.**

A plan of action is no guarantee of successful accomplishment, but an effective plan is built on detailed analysis and workable strategies. To provide more useful planning information, complete the next two columns of the Your Personal Financial Goals Worksheet (**WORKSHEET 20**) for each of your short-, intermediate-, and long-term goals. For each goal, assign a target achievement date and an estimated current cost. (You will determine the future cost later.)

Step 4: **Implement your plan.**

For many people, it is extremely difficult to override the tendency to spend what they have on what they want, no matter what the cost or consequence. And, most people haven't really thought too much about their goals or how much they will cost—especially future goals that must reflect changing prices or investment earnings over time. The foundation of financial planning is controlled spending—spending that balances the needs and wants of today and tomorrow—while still allowing you to accomplish your goals.

Step 5:   Review your progress, reevaluate, and revise your plan.

Remember your priorities!

Exercise 3   Financial Well-Being and Income Assessment

OBJECTIVES

By completing this part of Your Financial Plan, you will:
- Review your current financial record-keeping system.
- Develop a balance sheet.
- Complete the Income Statement Page in the Master Plan Calculator.
- Familiarize yourself with the Committed Expense Page and the Uncommitted Expense Page in the Master Plan Calculator.
- Complete the Uncommitted Expense Page in the Master Plan Calculator.

Step 1:   Evaluate your financial health.

Controlled spending—spending that balances the needs and wants of today and tomorrow—is the way to financial security. Controlled spending allows you to save to accomplish your goals by giving you insight into the amount of your available income, and matching that income to an expense plan that includes savings.

Step 2:   Define your financial goals.

In order to plan for your future financial goals, you should assemble a current and accurate record of your past finances. Review Chapter 2 and complete the Storing Financial Files Worksheet (**WORKSHEET 6**) to assist you with the remainder of Your Financial Plan.

Next, complete the Balance Sheet Worksheet (**WORKSHEET 4**) or the Net Worth Calculator (found on the text's Web site, **www.pearsonhighered.com/keown**) by inputting your current financial information. Complete either of these statements for "today," as that is your only realistic picture. Although your current net worth may not be indicative of your target year, the asset and debts you have accumulated today will follow you into your future.

Step 3:   Develop a plan of action.

You have just developed a picture of your financial past, and in Exercise 2 you built a picture for your future, so now it is time to concentrate on the present—your target year. Begin filling out the Income Statement Page of the Master Plan Calculator (found on the text's Web site, **www.pearsonhighered.com/keown**) by entering the projected target year income, including other sources of income that you researched in Exercise 1. Skip the Salary Reduction section of the income statement for now (you will complete this section in future parts of Your Financial Plan), but remember to include on the bottom of the statement any nontaxable income you expect to receive such as loans or gifts. The latter is an important consideration if you will be in graduate or professional school and receiving support from family, friends, or other sources.

NOTE: Selected information entered on the Income Statement Page of the Master Plan Calculator will automatically transfer to other pages.

Step 4:   Implement your plan.

Now complete the Uncommitted Expense Page of the Master Plan Calculator by researching, estimating, and recording expenses. Some of these costs may take some research. For example, you can estimate local food costs by using the federal per diem food rates for that locale; mass transportation rates are widely available through the local transit authority Web sites. The University of Michigan offers links to some very enlightening "living" costs, available at **www.lib.umich.edu/govdocs/steccpi.html**. Be careful to consider how changes in your lifestyle during your target year—such as dry cleaning or other costs that your parents may currently pay—will impact your expenses. Or, if you will be enrolled in graduate or professional school, be sure to include all education-related expenses.

The Uncommitted Expense Page and its companion, the Committed Expense Page, will serve as your guide through the rest of Your Financial Plan. Use the Uncommitted Expense Page to allocate your money to expenses that are more flexible and variable than those on the Committed Expense Page, which represent expense categories related to your financial security. You will complete the Committed Expense Page and the rest of the Master Plan Calculator as you finish subsequent exercises.

Please notice that as you enter either committed or uncommitted expenses, your "Total Income Remaining" recalculates. Refer to this number as you continue to incur "expenses," and note that you may need to adjust expense amounts later as you continue to develop you plan.

Step 5:   Review your progress, reevaluate, and revise your plan.

Remember your priorities!

Exercise 4   Tax Planning

OBJECTIVES

By completing this part of Your Financial Plan, you will:
- Estimate your federal, state, and Social Security tax liability.
- Determine your available income after taxes and disposable income for spending, saving, and investing.

Step 1:   Evaluate your financial health.

Determining how much income is really available to you after taxes, to spend, save, or invest, is a critical step in financial planning. As you implement your plans for pre-tax deductions for insurance and pre-tax deferrals for retirement in future exercises, be sure to (1) recalculate your state tax liability and (2) monitor the changes in disposable income.

Step 2:   Define your financial goals.

To estimate your tax liability, complete the Tax Form Page in the Master Plan Calculator (found on the text's Web site, **www.pearsonhighered.com/keown**). Once you enter your projected filing status and the number of your exemptions, you will need to project your itemized deductions and enter that amount or accept the standard deduction. For assistance, see Chapter 4. The worksheet will calculate your estimated federal and Social Security tax liability.

To research how to estimate your state taxes, visit **www.pearsonhighered.com/keown** for links to Internet sites to research how to estimate your state taxes, or visit the Web site of your state department of taxation. Take care to use the correct taxable "base" income for the calculation; some states base the state tax calculation on gross income while others use federal taxable income.

Step 3:   **Develop a plan of action.**

Based on the calculations in Step 2, your federal tax and Social Security/FICA taxes will automatically enter on the Income Statement Page of the Master Plan Calculator. However, you will need to manually enter your estimated state tax liability on line 43.

Step 4:   **Implement your plan.**

You have now completed the Tax Form Page and all sections of the Income Statement Page of the Master Plan Calculator except for the Salary Reduction for Employer-Sponsored Benefits section. This section will be completed in future exercises and will change your taxable income.

You now have an estimate of your disposable income for your target year. However, because you will adjust the salary reduction figures in subsequent sections to reflect your target year employee benefit costs and elective deferrals for retirement, you will need to monitor the changes in your disposable income.

Step 5:   **Review your progress, reevaluate, and revise your plan.**

Remember your priorities!

PART 2

Managing Your Money

Exercise 5   Cash Management and Short-Term Goal Planning

OBJECTIVES

By completing this section of Your Financial Plan, you will:
- Determine your cash management needs.
- Identify the cash management accounts you need.
- Complete the short-term goal section of the Your Personal Financial Goals Worksheet.
- Calculate the amount you need for your emergency fund and short-term savings goals.

Step 1:   **Evaluate your financial health.**

One of the most important short-term goals is the establishment of an emergency fund. Review the financial asset section of your Balance Sheet Worksheet (**WORKSHEET 4**) that you completed in Exercise 3, and identify the account(s) that you will designate for your emergency fund and other short-term goals.

Step 2:   **Define your financial goals.**

Consider goals that you hope to achieve within one year (or just a little more) of your target year as listed on the Your Personal Financial Goals Worksheet (**WORKSHEET 20**). (NOTE: If you have any debt reduction goals, bypass them for now; you will address them in Exercise 6.)

Research different types of accounts and their respective rates of return and, if applicable, compare the types of accounts you are currently using to other available alternatives. Visit **www.pearsonhighered.com/keown** to find links to Web sites that will help you research this information. Next, use the Money in Motion Calculator (found on the text's Web site, **www.pearsonhighered.com/keown**) to estimate the inflation-adjusted future cost of each goal on your desired achievement date, if applicable.

Step 3:   **Develop a plan of action.**

Develop a plan of action by matching your goal(s) to an appropriate cash management account. Next, decide which goals to fund and calculate the periodic savings requirement you need to achieve your goals. Then, enter the amounts in columns 5, 6, and 7 of the Your Personal Financial Goals Worksheet for each short-term goal.

Step 4:   **Implement your plan.**

Record your decision in your Master Plan Calculator (found on the text's Web site, **www.pearsonhighered.com/keown**). Enter the total annual savings amount for all your short-term goals and your emergency fund in the Savings/Investment Section on the Committed Expense Page.

Step 5:   **Review your progress, reevaluate, and revise your plan.**

Remember your priorities!

Exercise 6   Debt Management

OBJECTIVES

By completing this section of Your Financial Plan, you will:

- Analyze your projected debt situation.
- Review, reevaluate, and revise Your Financial Plan by making adjustments to planned spending or goals.
- Determine your planned debt payments (e.g., credit card, student loan, and auto loan).
- Determine your contractual payments (e.g., housing rental, auto lease, or telecommunication service contracts).

Step 1:   **Evaluate your financial health.**

There are two methods of debt load evaluation. First, review your credit report to verify your credit history. Second, calculate your financial ratios to diagnose current or potential credit problems.

Step 2:   **Define your financial goals.**

See Chapter 6 for information about receiving one *free* copy of your credit report or visit **www.pearsonhighered.com/keown** to find links to related Web sites.

Calculating the debt limit ratio is the most effective method to determine the level of monthly debt you should be able to handle. If you have or anticipate having any consumer credit payments (e.g., credit cards, student loans, installment loans for furniture or electronics, auto loans, etc.) during your target year, use the Financial Ratios Calculator (found on the text's Web site, **www.pearsonhighered.com/keown**) to compute your debt limit ratio. If you know that you will have credit payments during your target year, but do not know the amount of the payments, proceed to Step 3 to calculate the estimated payments. If you do not anticipate having or incurring any credit payments during your target year, enter "0" in the Debt Management Section of the Committed Expense Page in the Master Plan Calculator (found on the text's Web site, **www.pearsonhighered.com/keown**) and proceed to Exercise 7. Be sure not to overlook your housing payment in this section.

Step 3:   **Develop a plan of action.**

A. *If you plan to payoff, consolidate, or reorganize student loan debt*, talk to your lender, visit your lender's Web site, or go to **www.pearsonhighered.com/keown** for links to Web sites with student loan repayment calculators.

B. *If you anticipate having a balance on your credit card* from charges prior to or during your target year, go to **www.pearsonhighered.com/keown** for links to Web sites with credit card repayment calculators.

C. *If you anticipate making furniture, electronics, auto, or other purchases on credit* prior to or during your target year, go to **www.pearsonhighered.com/keown** for links to Web sites with amortized loan and credit line repayment calculators.

Review the Your Personal Financial Goals Worksheet (**WORKSHEET 20**) to determine if your short- or intermediate-term goals are reasonable given your current financial situation. Reconsider your goals or adjust the payments until your debt limit ratio is in a safe range.

Step 4:   Implement your plan.

Enter each credit payment in the Debt Management Section of your Committed Expense Page in your Master Plan Calculator. If your family, a friend, or other source has committed to assisting you with any of these payments, enter the planned assistance amount as a Nontaxable Gift on the Income Page in your Master Plan Calculator.

Step 5:   Review your progress, reevaluate, and revise your plan.

Remember your priorities!

Exercise 7   Large Purchase Management and Intermediate-Term Goal Planning

OBJECTIVES

By completing this section of Your Financial Plan, you will:
- Explore the feasibility of making a large purchase (e.g., auto, home, vacation home, etc.).
- Complete the intermediate- and long-term goal sections of the Your Personal Financial Goals Worksheet.
- Decide if the purchase is consistent with your other financial goals.
- Decide if you should postpone the purchase and, if so, calculate the amount of savings you need to accumulate a down payment.

Step 1:   Evaluate your financial health.

First, determine your asset availability by reviewing your monetary assets and determining the amount of money you need for a down payment. Second, determine your additional debt capacity by reviewing your financial ratios.

Step 2:   Define your financial goals.

Contemplate your ideal housing and transportation goals. How will such purchases affect your financial flexibility? Now compare your ideal housing and transportation goals with the most realistic scenario for the target year of Your Financial Plan. Determine how you might adjust your goals by reallocating existing funds, delaying the achievement date, or reducing the cost of your goals.

Step 3:   Develop a plan of action.

To develop a plan of action for making a large purchase in the future, consider the following steps:

A. Use the Money in Motion Calculator (found on the text's Web site, **www.pearson highered.com/keown**) to estimate the future purchase price of the auto or home, given a reasonable 3 to 5 percent inflation rate. Then, determine your projected down payment based on this price. To avoid private mortgage insurance, it will be important to make a minimum down payment of 20 percent for a home purchase. For an auto purchase, a down payment of 10 to 20 percent or more is reasonable.

B. Use the Money in Motion Calculator to estimate the annual savings you require given your projected time line. For intermediate-term goals with longer horizons, you can use the Portfolio Allocation Calculator (found on the text's Web site, **www.pearson highered.com/keown**) to determine stock-market-based historic rates of return for different diversified portfolios. The calculator will allow you to choose portfolios on the basis of your desired rate of return, your risk tolerance, and your time horizon criteria. For shorter-term goal achievement, it is more important to maintain the safety of the funds than the rate of return, so use Portfolios II or III to determine your expected return, or use the Money in Motion Calculator.

Repeat this process for each large purchase or intermediate goal. You may need to add a savings goal or complete the original savings goal on the Your Personal Financial Goals Worksheet (**WORKSHEET 20**).

Automobile purchase: Review Chapter 8 and complete the Lease Versus Purchase Worksheet (**WORKSHEET 9**). Use the Auto Loan Calculator (found on the text's Web site, **www.pearsonhighered.com/keown**) to determine your proposed auto payment. Now calculate the debt limit ratio or the long-term debt coverage ratio of this purchase on the Financial Ratios Calculator (the recommended limit is 2.5).

Housing purchase: Complete the Rent Versus Buy Worksheet (**WORKSHEET 10**). Now use the Worksheet for Calculating the Maximum Monthly Mortgage Loan for Which You Qualify (**WORKSHEET 11**) or, if you have a house price, use the Mortgage Loan Calculator (found on the text's Web site, **www.pearsonhighered.com/keown**) to determine your payment. Add in estimates for taxes and insurance (available on the real estate listing). Use the Mortgage Ratios Page of Financial Ratios Calculator (found on the text's Web site, **www.pearsonhighered.com/keown**) to complete the front-end and back-end mortgage qualification ratios. Is this purchase feasible? Finally, enter the payment into the long-term debt coverage ratio (the recommended limit is 2.5).

Complete columns 5, 6, and 7 of the Your Personal Financial Goals Worksheet or add a new goal to save for a down payment.

Step 4:   Implement your plan.

If you are adding or changing a savings goal, make the corresponding entry in the Savings/Investments Section on the Committed Expense Page in your Master Plan Calculator (found on the text's Web site, **www.pearsonhighered.com/keown**). If you will purchase either a car or a home, enter the projected payments in the Debt Management Section on the Committed Expense Page in your Master Plan Calculator.

Step 5:   Review your progress, reevaluate, and revise your plan.

Remember your priorities!

PART 3

Protecting Yourself with Insurance

| **Exercise 8** | Risk Planning |

> *OBJECTIVES*
> By completing this part of Your Financial Plan, you will:
> - Consider the decision to purchase insurance or self-insure.
> - Research the typical employer-provided benefits common to your career field.
> - Determine the amount of income available for insurance premiums.

Step 1: **Evaluate your financial health.**

The need for insurance arises from Principle 7: Protect Yourself Against Major Catastrophes. Determine the best insurance products and amounts of coverage.

Step 2: **Define Your Financial Goals**

If you are not currently employed in your chosen career field, research the employee benefits that it may offer to help you determine the types of insurance you may need and typical out-of-pocket costs. Keep in mind that benefit packages are not standard. To learn more about your chosen career field, consider the following ideas:

1. Identify someone working in the job or industry that you wish to enter—a friend, recent graduate in your major, or someone else you know—and discuss the benefits available and the associated costs, or ask if there is a company Web site or a personnel office that you might consult. Be sure to ask about an entry-level position.

2. Speak with your career advisor or visit the career services department on campus for information on benefits or suggestions for identifying someone in your career field.

Step 3: **Develop a plan of action.**

The reasons for self-insuring can be financial or ideological, but to truly self-insure you must make a conscious decision not to purchase insurance. After thorough analysis, it may be a viable and cost-effective alternative. Consider the short- and long-term consequences for yourself and all household members when considering your options for insurance.

Step 4: **Implement your plan.**

Review the Master Plan Calculator (found on the text's Web site, **www.pearsonhighered .com/keown**) to determine the amount of disposable income available to you for funding insurance premiums. Recognize that pre-tax premium payments will actually reduce your income tax liability, so monitor those changes in future exercises. Finally, review planned spending to determine where reductions may be made, if necessary.

Step 5: **Review your progress, reevaluate, and revise your plan.**

Remember your priorities!

| Exercise 9 | Protecting Yourself with Life Insurance |

OBJECTIVES

By completing this part of Your Financial Plan, you will:

- Evaluate the amount of life insurance coverage you need.
- Research the availability and annual pre-tax premium of the life insurance through your (or your spouse's) employer.
- Research the annual premium costs for the life insurance coverage you must purchase from a private insurance company.
- Research any available coverage purchased by your parents or others and any coverage that will continue for free.

Step 1: **Evaluate your financial health.**

Use Table 9.1 to determine if you, your spouse, or other family members require life insurance during your target year. Regardless of the outcome of the worksheet, if you have any debt that you do not wish to burden your survivors with, or if you do not have sufficient savings to pay for final expenses, you should seriously consider maintaining your employer-provided coverage. If you decide that you do not need *any* life insurance, skip to Step 4.

Step 2: **Define your financial goals**

Use the needs approach to calculate your life insurance needs. Complete the Estimating Life Insurance Needs Worksheet (**WORKSHEET 12**) to determine the appropriate amount of coverage. Repeat this step for other members of your household who provide financial support. If your current coverage is adequate, skip to Step 4.

Step 3: **Develop a plan of action.**

Once you have determined your life insurance coverage shortfall, you must select a policy. For this exercise, if purchasing an individual policy, you should assume that renewable term-life policies are appropriate. Consult several insurance agents or use the Internet sites at **www.pearsonhighed.com/keown** to price the appropriate amount of coverage for yourself or any other household members. (NOTE: To adequately protect yourself, err on the high side.)

Step 4: **Implement your plan.**

Implement your plan for your target year by purchasing the insurance and completing one of these steps:

A. *If you do not need any life insurance coverage*, enter "0" for the life insurance premium in the Insurance Premiums Section of the Committed Expense Page in the Master Plan Calculator (found on the text's Web site, **www.pearsonhighered.com/keown**).

B. *If your employer-provided life insurance coverage is adequate* and the premium is a pre-tax deduction from your salary, enter the premium in the Salary Reduction for Employer-Provided Benefits Section of the Income Page in the Master Plan Calculator. If you do not own an individual life insurance policy, enter "0" for the life insurance premium in the Insurance Premiums Section of the Committed Expense Page in the Master Plan Calculator.

C. *If you need to purchase additional life insurance or you will assume the premium for an existing policy*, enter the life insurance premium in the Insurance Premiums Section of the Committed Expense Page in the Master Plan Calculator.

D. *If you have an employer-provided policy and an individual or family policy*, be sure to enter both premiums.

Next, complete the Insurance Tracker Worksheet (**WORKSHEET 15**) to consolidate all of your insurance information for easy record keeping.

Step 5: Review your progress, reevaluate, and revise your plan.

Remember your priorities!

Exercise 10   Protecting Yourself with Health Insurance

OBJECTIVES

By completing this part of Your Financial Plan, you will:

• Evaluate your needs for health insurance coverage.
• Research the annual pre-tax premium costs for the health insurance coverage available through your (or your spouse's) employer.
• Research the annual premium costs of private health insurance coverage you must purchase if you are not employed or eligible for coverage.
• Research whether health insurance coverage from a parental policy will continue if you are enrolled full-time in graduate or professional school.

Step 1: Evaluate your financial health.

Review Chapter 9 to analyze your health care coverage options. Be sure to consider the premium, deductibles and co-pays, annual stop-loss limit, maximum lifetime coverage limit, and the need for supplemental dental or eye care coverage.

Step 2: Define your financial goals.

Evaluate the status of your current health insurance coverage. If your current health insurance is adequate, skip to Step 4. If you do not own health insurance or your current health insurance is inadequate, continue to Step 3.

Step 3:   **Develop a plan of action.**

Compare several types of health insurance policies. If you are generally healthy, a policy with a high deductible may make the premium more affordable. Ensure that the policy you choose is available in your chosen location. Consult several insurance agents or use the Internet sites at **www.pearsonhighed.com/keown** to research and price an appropriate health insurance policy for yourself or any other household members.

Step 4:   **Implement your plan.**

Implement your plan for your target year by purchasing the insurance and completing one of these steps:

A. *If your or your spouse's health insurance coverage is provided at work* and the insurance premium is deducted from salary, enter the premium in the Salary Reduction for Employer-Provided Benefits Section of the Income Page in the Master Plan Calculator (found on the text's Web site, **www.pearsonhighered.com/keown**). If you do not own an individual or supplemental health insurance policy, enter "0" for the health insurance premium in the Insurance Premiums Section of the Committed Expense Page in the Master Plan Calculator.

B. *If you own an individual or family policy* and your household does not require additional health insurance, enter your current health insurance premium in the Insurance Premiums Section of the Committed Expense Page in the Master Plan Calculator.

C. *If you are in graduate or professional school and are still covered by a parental policy*, enter "0" for the health insurance premium in the Insurance Premiums Section of the Committed Expense Page in the Master Plan Calculator.

D. *If you must purchase individual or family health insurance coverage* because you are not covered by an employer-provided or parental plan, enter your health insurance premium in the Insurance Premiums Section of the Committed Expense Page in the Master Plan Calculator.

Next, complete the Insurance Tracker Worksheet (**WORKSHEET 15**) to consolidate all of your insurance information for easy record keeping.

Step 5:   **Review your progress, reevaluate, and revise your plan.**

Remember your priorities!

Exercise 11   Protecting Yourself with Long-Term Disability Insurance

---

> *OBJECTIVES*
>
> By completing this part of Your Financial Plan, you will:
> * Evaluate your needs for long-term disability insurance coverage.
> * Research the availability of and annual pre-tax or after-tax premium for long-term disability insurance available through your employer.
> * Research the annual premium costs of long-term disability insurance available from a private insurance company.

Step 1:   **Evaluate your financial health.**

Review Chapter 9 to analyze your long-term disability insurance coverage options. Be sure to consider the definition of disability, the elimination period and your emergency fund, the percentage of salary replacement, the lifetime benefit limit, and the premium.

Step 2:   **Define your financial goals.**

Once you have determined your current disability insurance coverage status for your target year, you need to calculate the appropriate amount of coverage you need. Use the Worksheet for Estimating How Much Disability Insurance Coverage You Need (**WORKSHEET 13**) to determine the adequacy of your coverage. For this step, you will also need your most recent Personal Earnings and Benefits Estimate Statement (PEBES) from the Social Security Administration. If you do not have a PEBES, call (800) 772-1213 for your information or visit the Social Security Web site at **www.ssa.gov**. If your current disability insurance is adequate, skip to Step 4. If you do not have disability insurance or your disability insurance provided through your employer or an individual policy is inadequate, continue to Step 3.

Step 3:   **Develop a plan of action.**

Compare several types of individual long-term disability insurance policies. Consult local agents to discuss your needs or visit the Internet sites at **www.pearsonhighed.com/keown** to research and price a long-term disability insurance policy for yourself or any other household members. You may also want to contact your employer's human resources department for additional information.

Step 4:   **Implement your plan.**

Implement your plan for your target year by purchasing the insurance or deciding to self-insure, and completing one of these steps:

A. *If your or your spouse's long-term disability insurance is provided at work and the premium is deducted as a pre-tax expense from salary*, enter the premium in the Salary Reduction for Employer-Provided Benefits Section of the Income Page in the Master Plan Calculator (found on the text's Web site, **www.pearsonhighered.com/keown**). If there is other individually purchased disability coverage available, also enter its premium in the Insurance Premiums Section of the Committed Expense Page in the Master Plan Calculator. If none, enter "0."

B. *If your or your spouse's long-term disability insurance is provided at work and the premium is deducted as an after-tax expense from salary*, enter the premium in the Insurance Premiums Section of the Committed Expense Page in the Master Plan Calculator. If you do own an individual or supplemental disability insurance policy, add the premiums for the two policies and enter that amount in the Insurance Premiums Section of the Committed Expense Page in the Master Plan Calculator.

C. *If you or other members of your household own an individual long-term disability policy and do not require additional disability insurance*, enter the current disability insurance premium(s) in the Insurance Premiums Section of the Committed Expense Page in the Master Plan Calculator.

D. *If you or other members of your household must purchase disability insurance because you are not covered by an employer-provided plan*, enter your disability insurance premium in the Insurance Premiums Section of the Committed Expense Page in the Master Plan Calculator.

E. *If after consideration of the premium costs and other goals you decide not to purchase a long-term disability policy*, enter "0" for the disability insurance premium in the Income Page and the Committed Expense Page in the Master Plan Calculator.

Next, complete the Insurance Tracker Worksheet (**WORKSHEET 15**) to consolidate all of your insurance information for easy record keeping.

Step 5: **Review your progress, reevaluate, and revise your plan.**

Remember your priorities!

Exercise 12 Protecting Yourself with Long-Term Care Insurance

(Complete this section only if you are nearing or over the age of 50.)

OBJECTIVES

By completing this part of Your Financial Plan, you will:

- Evaluate your needs for long-term care insurance coverage.
- Determine the appropriate amount of coverage you need.
- Research the availability and annual pre-tax premium costs for the long-term care insurance coverage from your (or your spouse's) employer.
- Research the annual premium costs for the insurance coverage you must purchase from a private insurance company.

Step 1: **Evaluate your financial health.**

Review Chapter 9 to determine your coverage need and what type of policy would be adequate for meeting the expenses of a nursing home or other assisted living care. Be sure to consider the factors or ADLs (Activities of Daily Living) that would qualify you for benefits, the elimination period for the policy, the coverage of in-home or untrained care, the lifetime benefit limit, the premium, and the availability of other assets.

Step 2: **Define your financial goals.**

Once you have determined your current long-term care insurance coverage status, you need to calculate the appropriate amount of coverage based on your projected situation. If your current long-term care policy is adequate, skip to Step 4. If your long-term care insurance through your employer or an individual or family policy is inadequate, continue to Step 3.

Step 3: **Develop a plan of action.**

Compare several types of long-term care insurance policies. You will need to ensure that you target the policy to costs in your chosen location. Consult an insurance agent who is familiar with long-term care insurance or visit the Internet sites at **www.pearson highed.com/keown** to research and price a long-term care insurance policy for yourself or any other household members. You may also want to contact your employer's human resources department for additional information.

Step 4: **Implement your plan.**

Implement your plan for your target year by purchasing the insurance or deciding to self-insure, and completing one of these steps:

A. *If your or your spouse's long-term care insurance is provided at work and the premium is deducted as an after-tax expense from salary*, enter the premium in the Insurance Premiums Section of the Committed Expense Page in the Master Plan Calculator (found on the text's Web site, **www.pearsonhighered.com/keown**). If you own an individual or supplemental long-term care insurance policy, add the premiums for the two policies and enter that amount in the Insurance Premiums Section of the Committed Expense Page in the Master Plan Calculator. (NOTE: In some situations, the employer may pay for the long-term care insurance policy as a "free" employee benefit.)

B. *If you or your spouse owns an individual long-term care insurance policy and does not require additional insurance*, enter your current long-term care insurance premium(s) in the Insurance Premiums Section of the Committed Expense Page in the Master Plan Calculator.

C. *If you or other members of your household need long-term care insurance*, enter your insurance premium(s) in the Insurance Premiums Section of the Committed Expense Page in the Master Plan Calculator.

Next, complete the Insurance Tracker Worksheet (**WORKSHEET 15**) to consolidate all of your insurance information for easy record keeping.

Step 5: **Review your progress, reevaluate, and revise your plan.**

Remember your priorities!

Exercise 13   Protecting Yourself with Homeowner's or Renter's Insurance

> *OBJECTIVES*
> By completing this part of Your Financial Plan, you will:
> - Evaluate your needs for homeowner's/renter's coverage.
> - Determine the appropriate level of coverage and the need to customize the policy with riders.
> - Research the annual premium costs.

Step 1:   **Evaluate your financial health.**

Review Chapter 10 and consider a policy's deductible; ACV or replacement cost coverage; the need for riders, floaters, or extensions for otherwise limited coverage property (e.g., jewelry, artwork, firearms, or collections); inflation guard; and other policy features.

Step 2:   **Define your financial goals.**

To assess the adequacy and appropriateness of your coverage, complete the Personal Property Inventory Worksheet (**WORKSHEET 21**). Include the property you currently own and also project for property that you anticipate purchasing before or during your target year. Next, calculate the appropriate amount of coverage based on your target year situation. Do the limits of your coverage meet your insurance company's suggested requirement for your dwelling or contents? Finally, review Table 10.1 to assist you with your pricing decision.

Step 3:   **Develop a plan of action.**

Compare several types of homeowner's or renter's insurance policies for your projected target year residence and contents. Carefully match the policy coverage to your assets and customize the policy to protect any limited coverage property. You will also need to ensure that the policy you choose is available in and targeted to costs in your chosen location. Consult a local insurance agent, visit the Internet site of your current insurance carrier or any other major property and casualty insurance carrier, or visit the Internet sites at **www.pearsonhighed.com/keown** to research pricing information and coverage guidelines. As you consider prospective policies, review the Ways to Lower Your Home Insurance Costs Worksheet (**WORKSHEET 14**) for ideas to reduce your premium cost.

Step 4:   **Implement your plan.**

To implement the plan for your target year, enter the premium for homeowner's (only if not included in the mortgage payment) or renter's insurance in the Insurance Premiums section of the Committed Expense Page in the Master Plan Calculator (found on the text's Web site, **www.pearsonhighered.com/keown**). Consider purchasing umbrella insurance once you have accumulated a relatively sizable net worth to adequately protect your assets.

Next, complete the Insurance Tracker Worksheet (**WORKSHEET 15**) to consolidate all of your insurance information for easy record keeping.

Step 5:   **Review your progress, reevaluate, and revise your plan.**

Remember your priorities!

Exercise 14   Protecting Yourself with Auto Insurance

OBJECTIVES
By completing this part of Your Financial Plan, you will:
- Evaluate your needs for auto insurance coverage.
- Research the appropriate amount and type of coverage and the annual premium costs.

Step 1:   Evaluate your financial health.

Review Chapter 10 to determine the adequacy and appropriateness of your coverage and consider the coverage limits, deductible, number and age of household drivers, and premium.

Step 2:   Define your financial goals.

Calculate the appropriate amount of coverage based on your target year situation. Be sure that your coverage meets or exceeds the generally recommended 100/300/50 split-limit guideline. If your auto is financed through a lending institution, be sure that the limits of your coverage meet or exceed your lender's requirements. If you are unsure, consult your loan documents or your lender.

Step 3:   Develop a plan of action

Compare several types of auto insurance policies for your target year vehicle. You will also need to ensure that the policy you choose is available in and targeted to costs in your chosen location. Consult a local insurance agent, visit the Internet site of your current insurance carrier or any other major property and casualty insurance carrier, or visit the Internet sites at **www.pearsonhighed.com/keown** to research and price auto insurance and coverage guidelines for yourself or any other household members. Be ready to take advantage of all available discounts prior to pricing your prospective policy.

Step 4:   Implement your plan.

Enter your current or projected cost for the auto insurance premium(s) in the Insurance Premiums section of the Committed Expense Page in the Master Plan Calculator (found on the text's Web site, **www.pearsonhighered.com/keown**). Consider purchasing umbrella, or excess liability, insurance once you have accumulated a relatively sizable net worth to adequately protect your assets.

Next, complete the Insurance Tracker Worksheet (**WORKSHEET 15**) to consolidate all of your insurance information for easy record keeping.

Step 5:   Review your progress, reevaluate, and revise your plan.

Remember your priorities!

PART 4

Managing Your Investments

Exercise 15 Risk Tolerance and Asset Allocation

OBJECTIVES

By completing this section of Your Financial Plan, you will:

- Assess your personal risk tolerance.
- Familiarize yourself with different asset allocation strategies.
- Consider how your risk tolerance, time horizon, and asset allocation affect your rate of return on investments.
- Choose one or more asset allocation models to implement for your investment goals

Step 1:   **Evaluate your financial health.**

What are your investment goals? What is the time horizon for each goal? What is your financial risk tolerance? Your investment plan and your asset allocation model must accurately reflect the answers to these questions. A thorough understanding of your tolerance for risk and how it influences your investment decisions is a critical foundation for achieving investment goals.

Step 2:   **Define your financial goals.**

Take the online Risk Tolerance Quiz (found on the text's Web site, **www.pearsonhigher ed.com/keown**) to learn more about your investment attitudes. Do you agree with the results?

At first glance, an asset allocation model appears to be simple; however, it is a set of complex decisions built on your investment time horizon, financial risk tolerance, and the balance of investment risks with investment diversification. Asset allocation models are typically based on investing your savings in three major categories—cash, bonds, and equities—whether purchased directly or through mutual funds.

Step 3:   **Develop a plan of action.**

Go to the Portfolio Allocation Calculator (found on the text's Web site, **www.pearson highered.com/keown**), change the inputs, and compare the results. As you try different scenarios, consider your own situation. How will you balance risk tolerance and time horizon? Maintaining an appropriate balance among the asset classes within your portfolio is one of the objectives of asset allocation. Sticking to that asset allocation may require rebalancing the portfolio, perhaps annually, by selling and buying assets to maintain the original structure.

Step 4:   **Implement your plan.**

Choosing the right asset allocation model is critical to the success of your investment plan. To increase your chances of reaching your goals, be sure to tailor your portfolio to your investment time horizon, financial risk tolerance, and the balance of investment risks with investment diversification.

Step 5:   **Review your progress, reevaluate, and revise your plan.**

Remember your priorities!

Exercise 16   Long-Term Goal Planning

OBJECTIVES

By completing this section of Your Financial Plan, you will:

- Familiarize yourself with the current cost of your long-term lifestyle goals.
- Calculate, based on an assumed rate of inflation, the estimated future cost of your long-term lifestyle goals.
- Identify an average rate of return from a selected asset allocation model on the basis of your time horizon, risk tolerance, and investment style.
- Determine the required present savings needed to fund the estimated future cost of your long-term goals and the benefits of starting to save early.
- Determine the maximum amount, if any, that you can reasonably save for these goals during your target year.

Step 1:   **Evaluate your financial health.**

Review and evaluate your future savings needs for long-term lifestyle goals that utilize accounts that are not tax advantaged. Starting early means you can save less as you benefit from the effects of reinvested earnings.

Step 2:   **Define your financial goals.**

Use the Future Cost of Goals Calculator (found on the text's Web site, **www.pearson highered.com/keown**) to determine the future cost and savings requirement for each of your lifestyle goals. Complete the top section of the calculator to estimate the inflation-adjusted cost for each of your goals over the time horizon between your target year and your desired achievement date.

Step 3:   **Develop a plan of action.**

Review Chapter 11 and use the Portfolio Allocation Calculator (found on the text's Web site, **www.pearsonhighered.com/keown**) to determine which model portfolio best suits each goal. Use the rate of return from your chosen portfolio as the "expected rate of return" to complete the bottom section of the Future Cost of Goals Calculator. Next, complete the long-term lifestyle goals section of the Your Personal Financial Goals Worksheet (**WORKSHEET 20**) by completing columns 5, 6, and 7. If you will not be saving during your target year, leave column 7 blank.

Step 4:   **Implement your plan.**

If necessary, re-evaluate your long-term goals. Enter your total annual savings amount committed to all long-term goals in the Savings/Investment Section on your Committed Expense Page in your Master Plan Calculator (found on the text's Web site, **www.pearsonhighered.com/keown**).

Step 5:   **Review your progress, reevaluate, and revise your plan.**

Remember your priorities!

PART 5

Life Cycle Issues

Exercise 17 Retirement Planning

OBJECTIVES

By completing this part of Your Financial Plan, you will:

- Estimate the future cost of your retirement.
- Identify an average rate of return from a selected asset allocation model.
- Determine the required target year savings amount you need to fund the estimated future cost of your retirement.
- Compare the required target year savings amount you need to fund your retirement with the maximum amount that you can reasonably save for retirement during your target year.
- Decide if you will fund employer-provided retirement options, an IRA, or both.

Step 1: **Evaluate your financial health.**

Let's focus Your Financial Plan far into the future and start investing for retirement *now*.

Step 2: **Define your financial goals.**

To estimate your salary just prior to retirement, enter your target year salary and the number of years from your target year until you reach age 65 into the Retirement Planning Calculator (found on the text's Web site, **www.pearsonhighered.com/keown**). Complete the next two sections of the Retirement Planning Calculator by choosing your pre- and post-retirement asset allocation models. Change the scenarios on the Portfolio Allocation Calculator to develop your portfolios on the basis of desired rate of return, your risk tolerance, and your time horizon; for assistance, review Chapter 11. Use the Social Security Estimator (found on the text's Web site, **www.pearsonhighered.com/keown**) to determine your possible future benefits.

Enter your projected number of years in retirement (think about your family members' longevity to answer this question), your current retirement savings (Do you have any?), and, if applicable, your projected annual Social Security benefits to complete the Projected Retirement Savings Need section of the Retirement Planning Calculator. Now you have an estimate of the total savings you need to fund your retirement years as well as the required monthly and annual tax-deferred savings amounts. Enter your total savings needs at retirement, your expected tax-deferred rate of return, and your required annual savings in columns 5, 6, and 7 of the Your Personal Financial Goals Worksheet (**WORKSHEET 20**). (NOTE: If you are including a spouse or partner in your target year plans, you will need to complete this step again.)

Step 3:   **Develop a plan of action.**

Balance the target year Uncommitted Expense Costs in the Master Plan Calculator (found on the text's Web site, **www.pearsonhighered.com/keown**) with your long-term future costs for retirement.

Although just a rule of thumb, consider this simple approach.

- First priority, save enough in your employer-provided account to get the full match for the year. Don't pass up "free" money in the match!

- Second priority, assuming you can still afford to save more for retirement, fund an IRA.

- Third priority, if you can still save more, then invest the remaining balance in your employer-provided retirement account or in a non-tax deferred account to give you more goal flexibility.

Refer to the Retirement Planning Calculator to confirm your expected rate of return. Do the amounts you have chosen to save match the suggested total annual savings amount? Use the Internet sites at **www.pearsonhighed.com/keown** to estimate retirement benefits using different types of accounts.

Step 4:   **Implement Your Plan**

You may need to reconsider your priorities and review the results of Your Financial Plan. Implement your plan for your target year by committing to the retirement savings and completing one or more of these steps:

A. *If your employer offers a cash-balance plan or pension plan that is fully funded by the employer*, enter "0" in the Salary Reduction for Employer-Provided Benefits Section of the Income Page in the Master Plan Calculator.

B. *If your employer offers a retirement plan that you must fund with pre-tax salary deferrals or contributions to your employer-provided retirement account*, enter the amount in the Salary Reduction for Employer-Provided Benefits Section of the Income Page in the Master Plan Calculator. (NOTE: Enter only your contribution, regardless of the employer match. The employer match amount will be contributed to your retirement account, but will not be deducted from your salary.)

C. *If you choose to fund a Traditional or Roth IRA*, enter the annual after-tax contribution amount in the Savings/Investments Section of the Committed Expense Page in the Master Plan Calculator.

D. *If you choose to fund a taxable account to maintain flexibility for achieving other goals*, enter the annual after-tax contribution amount in the Savings/Investments Section of the Committed Expense Page in the Master Plan Calculator.

E. If you will be in graduate or professional school or are involved in a service activity that precludes sufficient income for *any* retirement investment, enter "0" in the Salary Reduction for Employer-Provided Benefits Section of the Income Page in the Master Plan Calculator and enter "0" in the Savings/Investments Section of the Committed Expense Page in the Master Plan Calculator. However, it will be important for you to consider the effects of waiting as illustrated in the Retirement Planning Calculator.

Step 5:   **Review your progress, reevaluate, and revise your plan.**

Remember your priorities!

Exercise 18 Education Funding Planning

> *OBJECTIVES*
> By completing this section of Your Financial Plan, you will:
> - Estimate the future cost of your child's education.
> - Identify an average rate of return from a selected asset allocation model.
> - Determine the required present savings needed to fund the estimated future cost of your child's education.
> - Compare the required present savings amount needed to fund the cost of education with your total target year savings amount, if any, for this goal.
> - Determine the maximum amount, if any, that you can reasonably save for this goal during your target year.

Step 1:   **Evaluate your financial health.**

Estimate the future cost of education.

Step 2:   **Define your financial goals.**

Determine the future cost of education. Use the information from the College Board's *Trends in College Pricing 2007* provided in the following table and the Future Cost of Education Calculator to estimate the inflation-adjusted cost of education for your child(ren).

Type of Institution	Average Tuition Cost	Increase (2007–2008)	Average Out-of-State Surcharge	Average Total Cost	Average Increase (2007–2008)
Two-Year Public	$2,361	4.2%	N/A	N/A	N/A
Four-Year Private	$23,712	6.3%	$10,455	$32,307	5.9%
Four-Year Public	$6,185	6.6%	$10,455	$13,589	5.9%

Be sure to match your cost estimate to the type of institution you chose and consider the percentage of education costs that you wish to fund.

Step 3:   **Develop a plan of action.**

Review Chapter 16 or visit the Internet sites at **www.pearsonhighed.com/keown** to learn more about college costs, savings plans, and loan repayment options. Determine if you will use taxable or tax-deferred accounts and an anticipated rate of return based on your risk tolerance, time horizon, and expected market conditions. Complete the Periodic Savings Requirement Calculator in the Future Cost of Education Calculator (found on the text's Web site, **www.pearsonhighered.com/keown**). Use the needed monthly savings amount to calculate the annual savings amount necessary to fund the estimated education costs.

Step 4:   **Implement your plan.**

Finally, repeat the steps above for each of your children, noting the type of institution you chose as well as the percentage of costs you wish to fund. Next, enter your total annual savings amount, or the amount that you can reasonably afford to invest, in the Savings/Investments Section of the Committed Expense Page in the Master Plan Calculator (found on the text's Web site, **www.pearsonhighered.com/keown**). Enter this amount only if your projected target year income is sufficient. If saving for your children's education was one of your goals, complete columns 5, 6, and 7 of the Your Personal Financial Goals Worksheet (**WORKSHEET 20**).

Step 5:   Review your progress, reevaluate, and revise your plan.

Remember your priorities!

Exercise 19   Estate Planning and Asset Transfer Planning

OBJECTIVES

By completing this section of Your Financial Plan, you will:
- Increase your awareness of the documents necessary to facilitate estate transfer.
- Increase your awareness of the documents necessary to establish control over end-of-life decisions in the event of medical incapacitation.
- If applicable, complete fundamental record keeping documents to facilitate estate transfer.
- If applicable, complete the worksheet to estimate your estate tax liability.

Step 1:   Evaluate your financial health.

Make and codify some basic decisions in estate planning.

Step 2:   Define your financial goals.

Estate planning goals focus on (1) property distribution and care for dependents; (2) estate preservation (by reducing taxes and settlement fees); and (3) control over end-of-life decisions.

Step 3:   Develop a plan of action.

1. Determine if you need a will, and if so, seek an inexpensive but valid method to prepare it. To learn about the intestacy laws in your target year state of residence, research how your assets would be distributed if you die without a will. Who would be responsible for administering your estate? Would someone be appointed by the court? If you are comfortable with this process, a will may not be necessary at this time. However, if you have a dependent(s), writing a will to establish a guardian(s) is a critical action.

2. Choose your heirs and decide what they will receive. Complete a Beneficiaries Contact Worksheet (**WORKSHEET 22**) to assist with the disposition of your estate. You may want to consider preparing a letter of last instructions, as explained in Chapter 17. Tell a family member or friend where your estate planning documents are stored.

3. Complete a living will, health care proxy, or advanced medical directive to give you control over end-of-life decisions. Research the documents and the requirements

(i.e., standard format allowed, number of witnesses required, etc.) in your target year state of residence. Acquire and review copies of the standard formats, if available, and when comfortable with the decisions, execute the forms. Tell a family member or friend about your wishes and the location of the documents. Please visit the Internet sites at **www.pearsonhighed.com/keown** to learn more about the tools of estate planning.

4. Review and complete the Estate Planning Worksheet (**WORKSHEET 23**) and the Assisting Parties Worksheet (**WORKSHEET 24**) to document your estate plans. Tell a family member or friend about your wishes and the location of the documents.

Step 4:   Implement your plan.

To determine if your estate or that of a family member is subject to federal estate taxes, complete the Worksheet for Calculation of Estate Taxes for the 2009 Tax Year (**WORKSHEET 17**). If the estate exceeds the tax-free threshold amount, visit an attorney to develop a more sophisticated estate plan. Additional legal assistance may also be necessary if you have a unique family or household situation that complicates the ownership or distribution of assets or the care needs of dependents.

Step 5:   Review your progress, reevaluate, and revise your plan.

Remember your priorities!

Using a Financial Calculator

Much of personal finance involves either determining how much you need to save to meet a future financial goal, or determining how big your payments will be on money you borrow today. All this finds its roots in **Principle 2: The Time Value of Money.** In fact, there's very little in personal finance that doesn't have some thread of the time value of money woven through it. With an understanding of the time value of money, we can compare dollar values from different periods.

With just a little time and effort, you'll be surprised how much you can do with a calculator, such as stripping away the effects of inflation and seeing what future cash flows are worth in today's dollars or what rate of return you are earning on an investment or paying on a loan.

In demonstrating how calculators make your work easier, you must first decide which calculator to use. The options are numerous and largely depend upon personal preference. We have chosen the Texas Instruments BA-II Plus.

In the examples that follow, you are told (1) which keystrokes to use, (2) the resulting appearance of the calculator display, and (3) a supporting explanation.

The keystrokes column tells you which keys to press. The keystrokes shown in an unshaded box tell you to use one of the calculator's dedicated, or "hard," keys. For example, if +/– is shown in the keystrokes instruction column, press that key on the keyboard of the calculator. To use a function printed in gray lettering above a dedicated key, always press the gray **2nd** key first, then the function key.

Here's what's coming:

Important Starting Point

Basic Time Value of Money Calculations
    A. Future Value
    B. Present Value
    C. Future Value of an Annuity
    D. Present Value of an Annuity

Loans
    A. Calculating the APR
    B. Calculating the monthly payment of a fixed-rate loan and the loan amortization

Calculating Future Values with Monthly Payments (Compound Sum)

Calculating the Number of Payments or Receipts

Calculating the Payment Amount

Calculating the Interest Rate

Bond Valuation
    A. Computing the value of a bond
    B. Computing the yield to maturity of a bond

AN IMPORTANT STARTING POINT

Example: You want to display four numbers to the right of the decimal.

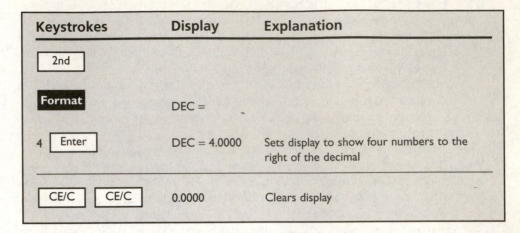

Keystrokes	Display	Explanation
2nd		
Format	DEC =	
4 Enter	DEC = 4.0000	Sets display to show four numbers to the right of the decimal
CE/C CE/C	0.0000	Clears display

Example: You want to set two payments per year to be paid at the end of the period.

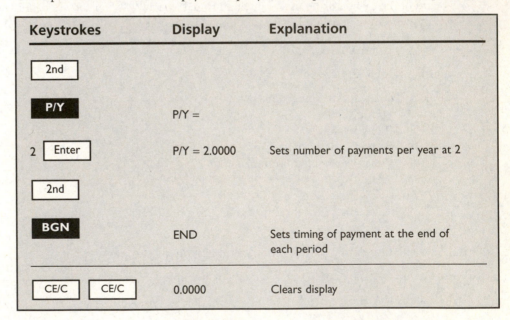

Keystrokes	Display	Explanation
2nd		
P/Y	P/Y =	
2 Enter	P/Y = 2.0000	Sets number of payments per year at 2
2nd		
BGN	END	Sets timing of payment at the end of each period
CE/C CE/C	0.0000	Clears display

BASIC TIME VALUE OF MONEY CALCULATIONS

A. The future value (Appendix A)

Example: Calculate the future value of $100 invested for 5 years at 12% interest rate.

Keystrokes	Display	Explanation
2nd		
P/Y	P/Y =	
1 Enter	P/Y = 1.0000	Sets number of payments per year at 1
2nd		
BGN	END	Sets timing of payments at the end of each period
CE/C CE/C	0.0000	Clears display
2nd		
CLR TVM	0.0000	Clears *TVM* variables
100 +/− PV	PV = −100.0000	Stores initial $100 as a negative present value. Otherwise the answer will appear as a negative.
5 N	N = 5.0000	Stores number of periods
12 I/Y	I/Y = 12.0000	Stores interest rate
CPT FV	FV = 176.2342	Calculates the future value

BASIC TIME VALUE OF MONEY CALCULATIONS *(continued)*

B. The present value (Appendix B)

Example: How much would you have to deposit in the bank today if you wanted it to grow to $8,000 in 8 years, earning 10% compounded annually?

Keystrokes	Display	Explanation
2nd		
P/Y	P/Y =	
1 Enter	P/Y = 1.0000	Sets number of payments per year at 1
2nd		
BGN	END	Sets timing of payments at the end of each period
CE/C CE/C	0.0000	Clears display
2nd		
CLR TVM	0.0000	Clears *TVM* variables
8000 FV	FV = 8000.0000	Stores future amount to be received
8 N	N = 8.0000	Stores number of periods
10 I/Y	I/Y = 10.0000	Stores interest rate
CPT PV	PV = −3,732.0590	Calculates the present value, which will be negative indicating a cash outflow

BASIC TIME VALUE OF MONEY CALCULATIONS *(continued)*

C. The future value of an annuity (Appendix C)
Example: What is the future value of $1,000 deposited at the end of each year for 15 years in an account earning 8% compounded annually?

Keystrokes	Display	Explanation
2nd		
P/Y	P/Y =	
1 Enter	P/Y = 1.0000	Sets number of payments per year at 1
2nd		
BGN	END	Sets timing of payments at the end of each period
CE/C CE/C	0.0000	Clears display
2nd		
CLR TVM	0.0000	Clears *TVM* variables
1000 +/− PMT	PMT = −1,000.0000	Stores annual payment (annuity) as a negative number. Otherwise the answer will appear as a negative.
15 N	N = 15.0000	Stores number of periods
8 I/Y	I/Y = 8.0000	Stores interest rate
CPT FV	FV = 27,152.1139	Calculates future value

BASIC TIME VALUE OF MONEY CALCULATIONS *(continued)*

D. The present value of an annuity (Appendix D)

Example: What is the present value of an annuity of $500 per year for 12 years at 9% annual interest rate?

Keystrokes	Display	Explanation
2nd		
P/Y	P/Y =	
1 Enter	P/Y = 1.0000	Sets number of payments per year at 1
2nd		
BGN	END	Sets timing of payments at the end of each period
CE/C CE/C	0.0000	Clears display
2nd		
CLR TVM	0.0000	Clears *TVM* variables
500 +/− PMT	PMT = −500.0000	Stores annual payment (annuity) as a negative number. Otherwise the answer will appear as a negative.
12 N	N = 12.0000	Stores number of periods
9 I/Y	I/Y = 9.0000	Stores interest rate
CPT PV	PV = 3,580.3626	Calculates the present value

LOANS

A. Calculating the APR

Example: Determine the annual percentage rate (APR) on a $6,000, 4-year (48-month) loan with monthly payments of $188.

Keystrokes	Display	Explanation
2nd		
BGN	END	Sets timing of payments at the end of each period
2nd		
P/Y	P/Y =	
12 Enter	P/Y = 12.0000	Sets 12 payments per year
CE/C CE/C	0.0000	Clears display
2nd		
CLR TVM	0.0000	Clears *TVM* variables
48 N	N = 48.0000	Sets *n*, the number of months for the investment
6000 PV	PV = 6,000.0000	Stores *PV*, the present value, which is the amount of the loan
188 +/− PMT	PMT = −188.0000	Stores *PMT*, the monthly payment (with a minus sign for cash paid out)
CPT I/Y	I/Y = 21.6813	Calculates *i*, which is the loan's APR

LOANS *(continued)*

B. Calculating the monthly payment on a fixed-rate loan and the loan amortization (the amount going toward principal and interest)

1. Example: What would be the monthly payment on a 15-year, $110,000 loan at a fixed rate of 8.5%?

Keystrokes	Display	Explanation
2nd		
BGN	END	Sets timing of payments at the end of each period
2nd		
P/Y	P/Y =	
12 **Enter**	P/Y = 12.0000	Sets 12 payments per year
CE/C **CE/C**	0.0000	Clears display
2nd		
CLR TVM	0.0000	Clears *TVM* variables
180 **N**	N = 180.0000	Sets *n*, the number of months for the investment (15 years × 12 months/year = 180 months)
110000 **PV**	PV = 110,000.0000	Stores *PV*, the present value, which is the amount of the loan
8.5 **I/Y**	I/Y = 8.5000	Stores *i*, the annual interest rate
CPT **PMT**	PMT = −1,083.2135	Calculates *PMT*, the monthly payment on the loan (with a minus sign for cash paid out)

LOANS *(continued)*

B. Calculating the monthly payment on a fixed-rate loan and the loan amortization (the amount going toward principal and interest)

Continuing with this example:

2. Example: On the sixtieth payment, what amount on the monthly payment goes toward interest and principal, and what is the unpaid balance on the loan?

Keystrokes	Display	Explanation
2nd		
Amort		
60 Enter	P1 = 60.0000	Sets beginning payment at 60
↓		
60 Enter	P2 = 60.0000	Sets ending payment at 60
↓	BAL = 87,366.0124	Calculates the unpaid balance when payment 60 is made
↓	PRN = −461.1048	Calculates the portion of payment 60 that goes toward the principal
↓	INT = −622.1087	Calculates the portion of payment 60 that goes toward interest

LOANS *(continued)*

B. Calculating the monthly payment on a fixed-rate loan and the loan amortization (the amount going toward principal and interest)

Continuing further with this example:

2. Example: Now you want to determine what portion of the total of your first 60 payments went toward interest and what portion went toward principal.

Keystrokes	Display	Explanation
2nd		
Amort		
1 Enter	P1 = 1.0000	Sets beginning payment at 1
↓		
60 Enter	P2 = 60.0000	Sets ending payment at 60
↓	BAL = 87,366.0124	Calculates the unpaid balance when payment 60 is made
↓	PRN = −22,633.9876	Calculates the portion of the first 60 payments that went toward the principal
↓	INT = −42,358.8224	Calculates the portion of the first 60 payments that went toward the interest

CALCULATING FUTURE VALUES WITH MONTHLY PAYMENTS (COMPOUND SUM)

Example: If you deposit $300 a month (at the beginning of each month) into a new account that pays 6.25% annual interest, compounded monthly, how much will you have in the account after 5 years?

Keystrokes	Display	Explanation
2nd		
BGN	END	Sets timing of payments at the end of each period
2nd		
SET	BGN	Sets timing of payments to beginning of each period
2nd		
P/Y	P/Y =	
12 Enter	P/Y = 12.0000	Sets 12 payments per year
CE/C CE/C	0.0000	Clears display
2nd		
CLR TVM	0.0000	Clears *TVM* variables
60 N	N = 60.0000	Stores *n*, the number of months for the investment
6.25 I/Y	I/Y = 6.2500	Stores *i*, the annual interest rate
300 +/− PMT	PMT = −300.0000	Stores *PMT*, the monthly amount invested (with a minus sign for cash paid out)
CPT FV	FV = 21,175.7613	Calculates the future value after 5 years

CALCULATING THE NUMBER OF PAYMENTS OR RECEIPTS

Example: If you wish to retire with $500,000 saved, and can only afford payments of $500 at the beginning of each month, how long will you have to contribute toward your retirement if you can earn a 10% return on your contribution?

Keystrokes	Display	Explanation
2nd		
BGN	BGN	Verifies timing of payment at the beginning of each period
2nd		
P/Y	P/Y = 12.0000	
12 Enter	P/Y = 12.0000	Sets 12 payments per year
CE/C CE/C	0.0000	Clears display
2nd		
CLR TVM	0.0000	Clears TVM variables
10 I/Y	I/Y = 10.0000	Stores i, the interest rate
500 +/− PMT	PMT = −500.0000	Stores PMT, the monthly payment invested (with a minus sign for cash paid out)
500000 FV	FV = 500,000.0000	Stores FV, the value we want to achieve
CPT N	N = 268.2539	Calculates the number of months (because we considered monthly payments) required to achieve our goal

CALCULATING THE PAYMENT AMOUNT

Example: Suppose your retirement needs were $750,000. If you are currently 25 years old and plan to retire at age 65, how much will you have to contribute at the beginning of each month for retirement if you can earn 12.5% on your savings?

Keystrokes	Display	Explanation
2nd		
BGN	BGN	Verifies timing of payment at the beginning of each period
2nd		
P/Y	P/Y = 12.0000	
12 **Enter**	P/Y = 12.0000	Sets 12 payments per year
CE/C **CE/C**	0.0000	Clears display
2nd		
CLR TVM	0.0000	Clears *TVM* variables
12.5 **I/Y**	I/Y = 12.5000	Stores *i*, the interest rate
480 **N**	N = 480.0000	Stores *n*, the number of periods until we stop contributing (40 years × 12 months/year = 480 months)
750000 **FV**	FV = 750,000.0000	Stores the value we want to achieve
CPT **PMT**	PMT = −53.8347	Calculates the monthly contribution required to achieve our ultimate goal (shown as a negative because it represents cash paid out)

CALCULATING THE INTEREST RATE

Example: If you invest $300 at the end of each month for 6 years (72 months) for a promised $30,000 return at the end, what interest rate are you earning on your investment?

Keystrokes	Display	Explanation
2nd		
BGN	BGN	Sets timing of payments to beginning of each period
2nd		
SET	END	Sets timing of payments to end of each period
2nd		
P/Y	P/Y = 12.0000	
12 Enter	P/Y = 12.0000	Sets 12 payments per year
CE/C CE/C	0.0000	Clears display
2nd		
CLR TVM	0.0000	Clears *TVM* variables
72 N	N = 72.0000	Stores *n*, the number of deposits (investments)
300 +/− PMT	PMT = −300.0000	Stores *PMT*, the monthly amount invested (with a minus sign for cash paid out)
30000 FV	FV = 30,000.0000	Stores the future value to be received in 6 years
CPT I/Y	N = 10.5892	Calculates the annual interest rate earned on the investment

BOND VALUATION

A. Computing the value of a bond

Example: What is the value of a bond that matures in 10 years and has a coupon rate of 9% (4.5% semiannually)? Your required rate of return is 12%.

Keystrokes	Display	Explanation
2nd **BGN**	END	Verifies timing of payments to end of each period
2nd **P/Y**	P/Y = 12.0000	
2 **Enter**	P/Y = 2.0000	Sets 2 payments per year and mode (END) assumes cash flows are at the end of each 6-month period
CE/C **CE/C**	0.0000	Clears display
2nd **CLR TVM**	0.0000	Clears TVM variables
20 **N**	N = 20.0000	Stores the number of semiannual periods (10 years × 2)
12 **I/Y**	I/Y = 12.0000	Stores annual rate of return
45 **PMT**	PMT = 45.0000	Stores the semiannual interest payment
1,000 **FV**	FV = 1,000.0000	Stores the bond's maturity or par value
CPT **PV**	PV = −827.9512	Calculates the value of the bond, expressed as a negative number

BOND VALUATION (continued)

B. Computing the yield to maturity

Example: What is the yield to maturity on a bond that matures in 8 years and has a coupon rate of 12% (6% semiannually)? The bond is selling for $1,100.

Keystrokes	Display	Explanation
2nd		
BGN	END	Verifies timing of payment to end of each period
2nd		
P/Y	P/Y = 12.0000	
2 Enter	P/Y = 2.0000	Sets 2 payments per year and mode (END) assumes cash flows are at the end of each 6-month period
CE/C CE/C	0.0000	Clears display
2nd		
CLR TVM	0.0000	Clears *TVM* variables
16 N	N = 16.0000	Stores the number of semiannual periods (8 years × 2)
1100 +/− PV	PV = −1,100.0000	Stores the value of the bond, expressed as a negative number
60 PMT	PMT = 60.0000	Stores the semiannual interest payment
1,000 FV	FV = 1,000.0000	Stores the bond's maturity or par value
CPT I/Y	I/Y = 10.1451	Calculates the yield to maturity, expressed on an annual basis